"Some years ago, I found myself astonished by the blog postings in *That's So Zen*. They were written by a young American woman living and training as a Zen priest in Japan. Then she wrote her first book, *Bow First, Ask Questions Later*, part memoir, part pointer to the Zen way, and I knew I was witnessing something rare. Gesshin Claire Greenwood brings her whole being to the project, leaving nothing out. Now, with her second book, *Just Enough*, she shows her continuing depth. And she invites us along. Here we get a taste of ancient Japan, monastic Buddhist Japan, Zen Japan, as embodied by a young twenty-first-century woman. East meets West. With nothing left out. Want a peek at the great way? Look at this book. Oh, and you get some very good recipes along the way."

— **James Ishmael Ford,** author of *Introduction to Zen Koans: Learning the Language of Dragons*

"*Just Enough* brings some Zen into your life with monastery-inspired vegan recipes, Buddhist sensibility, and a little sass oo. Gesshin Claire Greenwood serves up just enough."

— **Ellen Kanner,** soulful vegan author of the award-winning book *Feeding the Hungry Ghost: Life, Faith, and What to Eat for Dinner* (www.soulfulvegan.com)

Praise for *Bow First, Ask Questions Later*

sshin Greenwood is the real deal. That's what makes this book aluable. It's rare that someone from the West does any of this f, rarer still when they write about it, and yet even more rare their writing is as good as Gesshin's is. This is a truly unique ment of a truly unique lived experience."

— from the foreword by **Brad Warner,** author of *Don't Be a Jerk*

JUST ENOUGH

Also by Gesshin Claire Greenwood

Bow First, Ask Questions Later:
Ordination, Love, and Monastic Zen in Japan

JUST ENOUGH

Vegan Recipes and Stories
from Japan's Buddhist Temples

GESSHIN CLAIRE GREENWOOD

Foreword by Tamar Adler

Illustrations by Seigaku D. Amato

New World Library
Novato, California

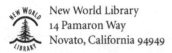

New World Library
14 Pamaron Way
Novato, California 94949

"Although the Wind," by Izumi Shikibu, translation by Jane Hirshfield with Mariko Aratani, © 1988 Jane Hirshfield, from *The Ink Dark Moon* (New York: Vintage Classics, 1990), used by permission of Jane Hirshfield.

Text design by Tona Pearce Myers
Interior illustrations by Seigaku D. Amato

Library of Congress Cataloging-in-Publication Data

Names: Greenwood, Gesshin Claire, author.
Title: Just enough : vegan recipes and stories from Japan's Buddhist temples / Gesshin Claire Greenwood.
Description: Novato, California : New World Library, [2019] | Includes index.
Identifiers: LCCN 2018052126 (print) | LCCN 2018058683 (ebook) | ISBN 9781608685837 (e-book) | ISBN 9781608685820 (print : alk. paper) | ISBN 9781608685837 (ebook)
Subjects: LCSH: Vegan cooking--Japan. | Veganism--Religious aspects--Buddhism. | Food--Religious aspects--Buddhism. | Cooking, Japanese. | Buddhist temples--Japan.
Classification: LCC TX837 (ebook) | LCC TX837 .G6742 2019 (print) | DDC 641.5/63620952--dc23
LC record available at https://lccn.loc.gov/2018052126

First printing, June 2019
ISBN 978-1-60868-582-0
Ebook ISBN 978-1-60868-583-7

Printed in Canada on 100% postconsumer-waste recycled paper

New World Library is proud to be a Gold Certified Environmentally Responsible Publisher. Publisher certification awarded by Green Press Initiative.

10   9   8   7   6   5   4   3   2   1

*This book is dedicated to women who feel
trapped in the kitchen, and to those who know
a pantry contains a universe of possibility.*

CONTENTS

FOREWORD

I tend to preface everything I write with epigraphs — small snippets of other people's writing. As though by proximity to their cleverness or wisdom or wit I can compensate for whichever of those virtues I lack. As though wallpaper could make a room sturdy.

After reading Gesshin Claire Greenwood's *Just Enough*, full of stories, rules, and admonitions about being a flawed person cooking and living in a flawed world, I found myself unable to lean on my old crutch. It seemed too hypocritical, in writing a few words of explanatory praise of her book — which is sturdy, wallpaper aside — to let myself off the hard task of writing new words about a new thing. I'm untethered. And it is refreshing.

This book is refreshing too. There isn't really that much in it. Without looking (because it feels fun not to) I think I can list the main ingredients in 90 percent of the recipes. They are burdock, daikon radish, carrot, shiitake mushrooms, bamboo, *konbu*, soy, miso, mirin, and sake. Cabbage shows up too.

What is there to say about bamboo and burdock, radish and the occasional cabbage? The chapter on bamboo is subtitled "Or, How to Turn Poison into a Meal." In addition to explaining

just how to correctly deal with each part of a bamboo stalk —
which must be harvested each spring in the Japanese mountains
to keep bamboo from invading and conquering the hillside —
it reminds a hurried reader how much better something tastes
when you've worked to make it palatable. "Many experiences
in life seem like unpeeled bamboo — inedible, ridiculous, ugly,
hard," Gesshin writes. "It is a step-by-step process. It takes time,
but it is not in and of itself difficult. First put the bamboo into a
pot. Then add rice bran and water. The difficulty is in renewing
our intention, in not giving up."

And in the section on miso there is a lesson that has
taught me, finally, the right amount of miso paste to add to
soup. It comes in a story about "the stink of Zen," which is, in
the author's words, "used to describe people who become obsessed with showing off their Zen practice or whose practice
is very loud and obvious to others." *Miso no miso kusaki wa
jyo miso ni arazu*, goes the Japanese proverb: "Miso that smells
like miso is not good miso." How much miso should I add to
dashi — which I keep trying and failing (and trying) to get
into a weekly practice of making? Enough to make it taste like
itself, but not overwhelmingly. In other words: *just enough*.

The recipes for Quick Japanese Cabbage Pickles and Marinated Fried Eggplant are ones to which I'll keep returning.
The reminder that in life and in food we "need a balance of
light and dark, just as we need a balance of flavors and a balance between discipline and abandon" is too.

And to me, as a lover of the bits and bobs at the bottom of
any pot; of the flotsam and jetsam of text that have been cut
out of articles; of the leaves, peels, stalks, stems, bones, roots,
peels, and other discards of animal and vegetable life; a book
that includes recipes for cooking with carrot peels and potato
peels and leftover curry is a welcome reassurance that we may
yet find a way to save what is precious.

— Tamar Adler, author of *An Everlasting Meal*
and *Something Old, Something New*

INTRODUCTION

A Zen riddle I often think about asks, "How can you drink tea from an empty cup?" I remember asking a monk in Japan this question. He smiled and said, "Empty cup is better than full cup, because you can always add to an empty cup." The odd paradox of using less is that sometimes it makes us feel even more satisfied. Becoming comfortable with lack can make us feel as though we have enough.

In my late twenties, I found myself in charge of running the kitchen at a Japanese convent called Aichi Nisodo, where I had lived for three years. I had come to Japan as a young, idealistic spiritual seeker and was hastily ordained in the Soto Zen tradition at age twenty-four — a decision I thought might help me solve my emotional problems (more on that later).

At Nisodo, nuns are placed in one of four work groups (kitchen, administration, chanting, and management), all run by senior nuns. For a period of three to six months, the novices learn the ins and outs of the specific work group, performing manual labor, cleaning, and obeying the commands of the woman in charge. At the end of the three- to six-month period, the nuns rotate to a different work group, so that everyone in the convent can learn and eventually master each area. The goal is that by the end of three or four years, each nun has been through each work group at least three times, making her qualified to lead it.

The first time I worked in the kitchen I was taught the basics. I learned how to wash rice, how to make Japanese soup, how to roast and grind *gomasio* (sesame salt). I spent hours cutting nori (dried seaweed) into thin strips to use as garnish, seeding pickled plums, and picking stones out of raw rice.

Nisodo's kitchen setup is unique among Japanese training monasteries, known as *senmon sodo* — institutions where Zen clergy go to complete the training that qualifies them to lead a temple. Whereas other monasteries have one head cook, called the *tenzo*, who supervises all meals, at Nisodo, the kitchen work group was responsible for planning the menu, shopping for food, taking care of the food pantry, keeping the kitchen clean, and prepping vegetables. However, the position of *tenzo*, or cook, rotated among the community daily, with the purpose of training everyone to make appropriate monastic food. Each and every trainee at Nisodo had a chance to be *tenzo* at least once a month. This is how I stumbled upon the rare blessing of learning Japanese monastic cooking from nuns — it was simply the required curriculum.

For the first year, every time it was my turn to cook, a Japanese nun was there watching my every move to make sure I didn't ruin things. By the second year I had a better handle on how to make food taste Japanese. I had learned the main methods of Japanese cooking — *itamemono* (frying), *sunomono* (marinating in vinegar), *nimono* (stewing), *takiawase* (mixing vegetables cooked separately), and *tsukemono* (pickling) — though I was not very skilled at any of them. By the third year I had learned enough that I could design menus and even teach the younger Japanese nuns how to make certain dishes.

Becoming proficient at cooking Japanese food was like adjusting the lens of a camera; it was a process of subtle focusing and readjustment. The biggest shift I had to make was in my relationship to flavor, especially soy sauce. As an American I had poured soy sauce onto rice, but I soon learned that Japanese food uses only a small amount of soy sauce. In Japan, good soup stock, timing, vegetable slicing, and salt, rather than bold flavors, inform the production of a good meal.

I approached learning to cook Japanese food with all guns blazing and no real understanding of the difference between Japanese, Chinese, and Korean food. I was used to dumping soy sauce and ginger onto everything. The first step in learning to cook Japanese food was listening — the willingness to learn. The second step was dialing back my natural impulse to overflavor things. I came to understand that if all steps in a meal are made with care and effort, a little soy sauce goes a long, long way.

In contemporary Western culture we don't pay much attention to that point in time when we have just enough. We're conditioned to think in terms of lack. Do I have enough money to retire? Enough friends? Am I exercising enough? This of course is not about having just enough, but about having *not* enough. We are usually making an assumption based on a comparison with the people around us. How much money we need to retire is relative; it depends entirely on what standard of living we're used to and what lifestyle we want to maintain. There's no such thing as too few or too many friends. Any idea about this would come from comparing our number to the perceived friend count of others. And of course, although everyone benefits from exercise, there's no predetermined universal amount that is sufficient for everyone.

The strange part about this kind of "not enough" thinking is that it usually results in overabundance or excess rather than just enough. Worldwide, the United States has the highest rate of consumer spending per household, the highest military spending budget, and the highest rate of obesity. We have 5 percent of the world's population, but use 23 percent of the world's coal. A recent study by Oregon State University indicated that for a woman in the United States, not having a child decreases her carbon footprint by twenty times that of other options like recycling or using energy-efficient household appliances. This is because living in the United States comes with a higher rate of resource consumption. I find this research fascinating; the best thing for an American to do for the environment is to not produce any more Americans.

What's more, in our culture, success is synonymous with not just the ability to make money, but the ability to buy the right things at the right time. And yet anyone who has felt the emotional toll of earning and spending knows that there is only limited happiness to be found in purchasing the right thing. This is not to say that there's no pleasure in buying things — of course there is!

I love the moment in the movie *Before Sunset* when the female protagonist is chatting with Ethan Hawke on the train. She says: "I feel really alive when I want something more than just basic survival needs. I mean, *wanting*, whether it's intimacy with another person or a new pair of shoes, is kind of beautiful....It's okay to want things as long as you don't get pissed off if you don't get them."

There is indeed a kind of aliveness that comes with wanting, but remaining balanced and moderate with desire is easier said than done. What Buddhist philosophy and practice point to is the understanding that our desires are insatiable — that there is never an end to what we want to be, have, buy, or accomplish.

Does this sound familiar? You want the new iPhone; you suffer because you don't have it, and so you buy it. But then the phone breaks, or Apple comes out with a new model and

you want that. This is how the consumer economy continues
to flourish. This is how the cycle of birth and death continues;
we want someone, we can't have them, we get them, and then
we procreate, or adopt, or buy a nice piano instead. As poet
Walt Whitman pointed out, human existence is defined by
wanting: "Urge and urge and urge," he wrote in *Song of Myself,
III*. "Always the procreant urge of the world."

And yet it's too simple to say, "Wanting is bad." I was ordained as a Buddhist nun when I was twenty-four years old
and spent most of my twenties in monasteries in Japan. At
first I was attracted to Buddhism because of the meditation
practice; it offered me a sense of calm and sanity in the midst
of my stressful, chaotic college years. Soon I came to admire
Buddhism's sophisticated ethical system and the emphasis on
simplicity and minimalism. As someone raised in a well-off
family, I found the notion of not having or going without
revolutionary. However, my time in the monasteries in Japan
taught me that Buddhism is not simply about going without,
minimalism, or scarcity. It stresses what the Buddha called the
"middle way," a lifestyle between deprivation and excess.

According to legend, the Buddha was a prince, born into
a royal family. Trying to shield him from reality, the Buddha's
father gave him everything he wanted: fine clothing, the best
food, and beautiful women. However, one day the Buddha left
the palace and saw around him sickness, old age, and death.
He was then inspired to understand the truth, and he left the
palace in search of the end of suffering. For seven years he
practiced meditation and asceticism, eating only one grain of
rice a day. Due to this severe lifestyle, he became frail and sick
and almost died. Luckily, a girl from a nearby village saw him
and offered him a bowl of milk. Although in the past he had
sworn off milk and other rich foods, at this moment the Buddha drank the milk and felt reenergized. With his newfound

strength, he was able to sit and watch his mind long enough to come to understand the causes and conditions of suffering.

This story is the first example of the "middle way." Initially, the Buddha was a prince. He had everything he wanted and more — excessive amounts of food and riches — but still he was not happy. I think the story of the Buddha appeals to people in developed countries because, if we have our basic needs met, we often are in the same predicament. Trying to counteract this excess, the Buddha fasted and became sick. However, only when he found a middle way between extreme wealth and poverty, between sensual pleasure and self-mortification, was he able to end his suffering. This story can be important guidance for us.

A few years ago I read of a study by Princeton University that showed that money *does* buy happiness, but only up to a certain point. Researchers found that people who made below $75,000 per year felt more stressed and weighed down by everyday problems and that for those approaching the $75,000 per year mark these feelings lessened. However, making more than $75,000 per year did not make people feel happier. In other words, having enough food, objects, and money does make us feel better, but having more than enough doesn't.

What if we could retrain ourselves to think in terms of "just enough" rather than "not enough"? And what is this $75,000 amount per year about? For someone in a developed country, $75,000 might be just enough, but for the majority of the world's population, this amount of money is a fortune. In other words, our sense of what is "just enough" depends in large part on our surroundings, on what we are used to and expect. For some Westerners, finding the sweet spot of "just enough" will mean scaling down.

For Americans, experiencing "just enough" when we eat will often mean preferring the riddle's "empty cup" by eating less. But I believe this can — and should — be done with joy, grace, and pleasure. There is a beauty in just the right amount of anything: too much furniture in a room gives it a cluttered feeling, but not enough furniture means you can't sit down. This is not some kind of mystical Eastern concept either! All good painters know the importance of negative space — the artist Kara Walker's paintings are famous exercises in negative space, and what would Vermeer's *Girl with a Pearl Earring* be without that black background? With regard to food, there are ways to eat and cook that bring us closer to this philosophy of "just enough."

This book is many things. First and foremost, it is a cookbook. This book stems from the recognition that there are very few good cookbooks on vegan and vegetarian Japanese food in English. I lived in Japan between 2010 and 2016, many years of which were spent learning to cook in Zen monasteries. This book is meant to teach people the techniques and skills needed to cook food like the kind I ate in monasteries in Japan. For this reason, I have included a glossary listing common Japanese ingredients, useful equipment, and popular Japanese cooking techniques, which can be found at the end of the book.

But this book is also about balance, about discovering what is just enough — in cooking and in life. It is about the process, poetry, and meaning of food. In cooking, it is important to understand the right amount of things — the right amount of time, the right amount of salt, and the right amount of mixing. As we become better cooks, we become more attuned to how much yeast is necessary to make bread rise, how much seasoning to use, how many chili peppers are too many, how much oil is too little oil. Without an understanding of sufficiency and balance, there can be no good cooking.

But beyond food, I am also interested in what "just enough" means more broadly, what it means to live a life that is sane and balanced, a life that does not devolve into extremes.

This interest, of course, arose out of my personal experience living a comfortable childhood followed by a monastic life for many years that was austere and characterized by extreme self-denial. Coming out of that experience of extremes, I knew that, though the strict monastic path was beautiful and stressed many useful and important things, I wanted to find a more radical kind of balance.

The very first sermon of the Buddha is the teaching of the "middle way," because this process enabled his awakening. As I enter my thirties, I am just beginning to learn a good balance between wealth and simplicity, relaxation and rigor, greed and selflessness. The writing in this book shares my challenges and discoveries as I find this "middle way" in all areas of my life.

As I dove into researching Japanese food and testing recipes for this book, there was one issue I could not shake, a problem that quite literally woke me up in the middle of the night. This was the problem of "cultural appropriation." This term has a range of definitions, but it most often means (1) the act, by dominant racial groups, of profiting from the cultural products of an oppressed group in a way the oppressed group cannot, and/or (2) the adoption of cultural products from an oppressed group in a way that is disrespectful, unwanted, or uninvited.

It is a nuanced problem, one that white people especially are often loath to address. This is, I think, because we are afraid we might have to give up the beloved cultural products we have appropriated: Mexican food, Indian textiles, yoga, and so on. The thinking is that "nobody owns culture," that culture always moves and adapts in a dynamic process. This is of course true — culture does move and change — but, given the rise in racism, xenophobia, and homophobia in the past few years, I think it is our duty to examine how power and privilege operate rather than continue with business as usual.

Cultural appropriation is not really about who is allowed

to appreciate culture, but about who profits from it. Many people noted the hypocrisy of US Secretary of Homeland Security Kirstjen Nielsen's dining at a Mexican restaurant the same week she defended the administration's policy of separating immigrant families at the border. Within the web of white supremacy, even innocuous actions like eating — and access to certain kinds of food — become signs of power and privilege.

As a white person writing a book on Japanese food, I do not really know what to do about this. I feel an impulse welling up to defend myself — to argue that I am not *really* writing about Japanese food, but about a philosophy of "just enough," or to point out that these recipes and techniques were taught to me by Japanese nuns who wished to spread knowledge of their culture — but I'm not sure what such a defensive move would accomplish.

The truth is I do have the privilege of a platform. I often wonder if the reason so many white people have a problem with the concept of racial privilege is that we have a problem experiencing gratitude. We believe that our suffering makes gratitude irrelevant. But gratitude can and should exist regardless of conditions. It was Buddhist nuns who taught me that gratitude depends on our mindset, not on what we have.

"Privilege" is just that — a privilege. It is access to opportunities and resources that others do not have. I am grateful for the opportunity I had to learn about Japanese food from Buddhist nuns, to publish what I have written about things that matter to me, to have had an education that allowed me to write well, navigate the publishing industry, travel, and learn the Japanese language. And I am continually attempting to rebalance power and resources the best I know how, although my efforts in this area are probably insufficient; there is much more to say about shame, power, and whiteness, but perhaps that is a different book altogether.

I hope that the Japanese nuns (and some monks) who taught me these recipes — who held my hand and painstakingly explained, in both English and Japanese, the basics of Japanese cooking techniques; who taught me how to wash rice, treat bamboo, stew vegetables, season soup, slice green onions, and design meals that are balanced and delicious — are proud of this book. It would not have been possible if they hadn't been patient with a cocky young American who used too much soy sauce.

I am grateful and hope I have made them proud.

ZEN COOKING
BASICS

Here are some things to remember as you prepare the dishes in this book or any other meals you are making.

1. Treat vegetables as though they were your own eyes — be careful with them, take care of them, and don't touch them without washing your hands first.
2. Treat pots and pans like your own head. Same idea.
3. Understand the different cooking times of vegetables. Carrots cook slower than cabbage, so they need to be added to the pan first. Also, the larger the cut of vegetable (for example, with potatoes), the longer it will take to cook it. Green onions shrink and darken with heat, so if they are sliced thinly, they don't need to be cooked at all. If making soup, greens such as spinach or *komatsuna* don't need to be cooked either; they will wilt sufficiently in the scalding broth. Plan your cooking according to the cooking times of your ingredients.
4. Slice things with care. It's nice to have all the vegetables cut the same size or at least the same shape, for example, all in slices or all in rounds.

5. Prepare all your ingredients beforehand. It is tempting to start cooking before all the things are chopped, but this will just make you feel rushed.

6. Be brave with salt! My rule of thumb is to add salt until, when you taste the food, your brain tells you, "Yum. I want to eat more!" It's like going to Europe or falling in love — you'll know when you get there. At the same time, it can be scary to add enough salt. Restaurant cooks will tell you that everyone underestimates how much salt (and sugar, but that's another story) goes into restaurant food. But salt is not bad for you. Research has shown that high salt content is only dangerous for people who already have high blood pressure or kidney disease.

7. As in love, timing is everything. Serve hot food hot and cold food dressed at the last minute. Cook vegetables just the right amount of time. This sounds basic, but it is one of the hardest parts about cooking. You need to be in tune with what you are cooking. Watch closely and smell. Look for that color as vegetables brown. Dress your salad immediately before serving, not ten minutes before, or it will be soggy. If you are serving soup and another dish, make the soup first and then the other dish. Immediately before serving, bring the soup back to a boil, and only then add the garnish. If making several dishes, understand which foods cook fastest and make them last.

8. Store cooking tools in places that make sense. Heavy pots should be stored in low places, spoons and chopsticks in higher places. Clean up afterward.

9. Cook to nourish people and make them happy. Bring to mind those you are cooking for before you begin. Try to bring them joy with your food.

10. Basically, pay attention, understand and respect your materials, cook things the right amount of time, add just enough salt, and cook to nourish others.

ORYOKI

The Practice of "Just Enough"

W hat does it mean to have "just enough" — just enough taste, just enough flavor, just enough love? Zen monks throughout Japan learn an eating style known as *oryoki*. This word combines the Chinese characters for "receive," "amount," and "bowl," but overall it connotes a sense of "just enough" or the "right amount." The Zen ritual of *oryoki* has much to teach us about eating economically and well.

Dogen Zenji, the thirteenth-century founder of the Japanese Soto Zen tradition, in which I trained, wrote a cooking manual called the *Tenzo Kyokun*, or *Instructions for the Cook*. The *Tenzo Kyokun* lays out in detail what should be done during each hour of the day in the kitchen. Contrary to what you might expect, the instructions begin not in the morning, but the day before. To this day, monastery cooking begins the day before the meal with the preparation of vegetables and the washing of rice.

In the kitchen work group, one nun designs the next day's meal and sees that the more difficult and time-consuming vegetables are prepped — boiling bamboo, for example, or peeling potatoes — and placed in bins neatly labeled "Breakfast," "Lunch," and "Dinner." In the evening the assigned *tenzo* (or "cook") for the next day comes to the kitchen. This nun kneels on the ground and bows, asking politely to be informed about the menu. The nun in charge of the menu bows back and then explains what will be cooked. The cook is then given three meals' worth of vegetables and rice soaking in water for the next morning's breakfast porridge.

In the morning, the cook awakens with everyone else. She attends the first period of zazen, or Zen meditation, at 4:00 AM in the meditation hall with the community. She leaves after the first bell and changes out of her robes and into work clothes. In the predawn quiet she moves quickly to the kitchen and turns on the heat under the rice porridge. She fills a large pot with water and places this on the stove as well. As she begins cooking the breakfast vegetables, from the main Buddha hall she hears the familiar swell of women chanting to the rhythmic beat of a wooden mallet interspersed with the gonging of a giant bell. With the first boiled water of the day, she makes a small pot of green tea and places a cup of this on an altar for the god of the kitchen, Idaten.

Eventually the chanting in the Buddha hall ends and the relative quiet is broken by dozens of nuns rushing off to begin their morning cleaning tasks. The convent is alive with sound and activity. In the midst of it all, the cook cannot afford to be distracted, because, without her, there will be no food for the community. Thirty minutes before breakfast begins, she sounds a flat gong called the *umpan* to signify that the meal will begin soon. She busies herself with the finishing touches of breakfast, making sure there are enough pickles and that the table is set properly, and then darts out to hit the *umpan* again at ten-minute intervals.

The very last thing to do is scoop the rice porridge from the pressure cooker into a *handai* (or *sushi oke*), a bamboo basket for serving. While she does this, a younger nun sticks her head in to ask if she should assume her position at the drum across the monastery, for they will soon engage in a call-and-response bell routine to signify the beginning of the meal. The cook instructs her to go to the drum and then continues spooning the steaming porridge into the basket.

Once this is completed, she goes again to the *umpan* and hits it in steady strikes, gradually increasing speed until the whole hallway reverberates with her lightning-quick rhythm. She ends with one last strike signifying the beginning of the meal — and then hears the thump of the drum across the way in response, as the younger nun begins her part. This drum beats a sequence that all the experienced nuns recognize. At the final drumbeat, the nun sitting at the head of the table strikes two wooden clackers together. At this sound, everyone puts their hands together in *gasho*, the prayer mudra, and begins chanting.

Monastery work reminds us that no person exists in isolation. Each sound is a signal instructing the community, and often three or four people are involved in a sequence of drums, gongs, and bells. Making a mistake at any point can throw off the whole sequence. Over the years of participating in these sequences, you learn to pay attention to your actions and understand the consequences they have on others. You begin to embody the truth that we are at all times interconnected with the world around us.

Oryoki, the eating ritual practiced in Japanese monasteries, varies slightly between breakfast, lunch, and dinner. Special *oryoki* bowls (usually three to five black bowls nested inside each other) are kept wrapped in a gray cloth, with chopsticks and spoons in a cloth case on top. Traditionally, monks keep these bowls hanging on hooks above their beds in the meditation hall.

At Nisodo, we only ate in the meditation hall during *sesshin*, or weeklong intensive meditation periods. Most of the time we would eat sitting on the floor at a long wooden table in the dining room. The table was the oldest piece of equipment in the convent — over a hundred years old, and it bore scratches and nicks from generations of use. After a verse of chanting, we untied the cloth wrapping and opened our bowls. After opening the bowls and placing them on a black placemat, we chanted again.

> We reflect on the effort that brought us this food and
>   consider how it comes to us.
> We reflect on our virtue and practice, and whether we
>   are worthy of this offering.
> We regard it as essential to free ourselves of excesses
>   such as greed.
> We regard this food as good medicine to sustain our life.
> For the sake of enlightenment, we now receive this food.

At breakfast, our largest bowl was for rice porridge, and we would pass our bowls to the center of the table, where nuns spooned hot porridge into them. The middle bowl held cooked vegetables, if they were available, or simply pickles. If we had vegetables, we would pass the serving bowls of vegetables down the table and serve the person across from us, an abbreviated version of the more complex serving procedures that took place during meals in the meditation hall. At lunch, the large bowl again held rice, the middle bowl was for soup, and the third bowl held vegetables. Custom varies between monasteries throughout Japan, but in general breakfast is rice porridge, pickles, and sesame seeds; lunch is somewhat larger, with rice, soup, one or two vegetable dishes, and pickles; and dinner consists of leftovers — often vegetables mixed with noodles or rice.

After the meal was finished, we would clean our bowls by wiping them with a tool called a *setsu*, a stick with a piece of cloth attached to the end like a spatula. After wiping we licked leftover food from the *setsu* to make sure nothing was left in the bowls. Then we washed the bowls, first with tea (to loosen sticky rice grains) and then with hot water, carefully washing the smaller bowls and chopsticks in the middle bowl. No soap or additional washing was needed, because the food was usually made without oil and all the leftover food was consumed or wiped clean. At other monasteries, monks would use a pickle to clean their bowls instead of the *setsu*. It is said that pickles have antiseptic properties, which also helps the cleaning process.

Oryoki means "just enough" for two reasons. The first is that, in the ceremony of *oryoki*, all physical movement is prescribed and ritualized. For example, there is a form for exactly how to open your bowls (not only the order, but which fingers to use), how to hold the bowls when you eat, how and when to bow, which hand to use when wiping your bowls, and so on. This means that ideally you will always be using just the right amount of physical effort. In the beginning it is quite difficult to memorize all the minute details and rules of *oryoki* practice, but after a few months it becomes muscle memory. This enables you to eat without thinking. However, it is not a mindless, spaced-out kind of nonthinking. It is a nonthinking that is intimately attuned to the present moment.

Learning *oryoki* practice is intimidating. There is a strict way to do everything, and because no one talks during the meal, it can seem as though everyone is staring at you, waiting for you to make a mistake. Even Japanese people struggle to learn the elaborate form. It is also physically unwieldy at times; the bowls are slippery and the chopsticks flimsy between your fingers. In a quiet meditation hall, dropping chopsticks on the floor makes a sound like a cannon booming.

But I loved this practice. Some of the best meals I have ever eaten have been simple meals of rice, soup, and vegetables, eaten in silence. When eating occurs this way, the flavors come alive. Despite the small bowls of food, I feel satisfied. I stand up from the meal ready to move on, not craving dessert or to keep eating.

The second reason *oryoki* means "just enough" is because meals and portions are designed to be just enough to sustain life, yet also satisfying and delicious. One line monks chant before a meal is, "The five colors and six tastes of this meal are offered to dharma and sangha" (*dharma* means "truth," and *sangha* is the community of monks and nuns). The monastery cook is trained to pay attention to the five colors (white, yellow, green, red or orange, and brown/black or purple) and six tastes (sweet, salty, sour, bitter, spicy, and delicate). In contemporary Japanese kaiseki cooking (traditional high-end multi-course meals), most chefs will design meals with five flavors — sweet, salty, sour, bitter, and umami (a special savory taste; see chapter 3) — not six. But whether five flavors or six, a Japanese meal is tastefully balanced, not emphasizing one taste, such as sweet, at the expense of others. This balance of flavors makes people feel more satisfied after eating.

Observers of Japanese and Western culture often note that in the West we usually eat a lot of food piled on one plate, whereas in Japan people eat from several bowls during a meal. This has its roots in *oryoki* practice and also results in increased satisfaction after eating. Because in *oryoki* food is served in three to five small bowls, you must pick up each dish and give it your full attention while eating. When you want to try another dish, you have to set the first bowl down and then use two hands to pick up the second bowl. This takes time and attention, so you focus more on the sensations of eating rather than eating as much and as quickly as possible from one plate.

Recent scientific research has shown that because of the Delboeuf illusion, people feel more satisfied when eating from smaller plates and bowls. The Delboeuf illusion is an optical illusion in which, when two circles of equal size are placed next to each other, the one inside a larger circle appears bigger.

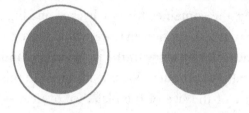

In *oryoki*, then, small amounts of food are placed in many bowls rather than on one large plate. Because of the ratio of food to bowl, this relatively small amount of food seems like a lot. Many factors, such as variety of flavors and colors, the use of multiple bowls, and plating strategies, contribute to the satisfaction gained from the *oryoki* style of eating.

I don't think the Buddhist monks in China who first started doing *oryoki* practice knew about the Delboeuf illusion, at least not by that name. They probably didn't care about portion control the same way dieters do. But I do think that they cared very deeply about the nature of desire and contentment — after all, this is the focus of Buddhist practice — and so *oryoki* naturally arose out of an understanding of the importance of "just enough." Outside of the monastery, it is very difficult to eat in the *oryoki* style; it is highly ritualized and relies on the communal nature of the practice, in which participants have assigned cooking and serving functions. However, I believe that we can carry the spirit of "just enough" into our meals and our lives.

In *oryoki*, we use many small bowls with small amounts of delicious food, and this makes us, paradoxically, feel more full. Quite literally, then, we can design our meals to reflect these principles by using more plates and smaller amounts of food with a wide variety of flavors and colors. In other words, we can change the *container* of our food to feel more satisfied. Broadly and metaphorically, this strategy can be brought into the larger frame of our lives. We can shift the "container" of our lives, so that no matter how much we have or do not have, it is enough.

Usually, the container for our lives is one big plate. The container is an expectation that we will make a great deal of money, have a lot of sex with the right people, and consume the right cultural products. We pile things onto this big plate, but because of the size of the plate, we overeat — we work more, buy more things, have more sex. And yet we don't feel satisfied. If we were to change bowls, if we were to reframe our value system, then we could see our lives through a different perspective. If we bring awareness to the present moment, if we value wisdom and compassion more than material acquisition, then our lives will always feel full. They will feel full, because all that we need is awareness and the cultivation of wisdom. Within this container of awareness, wisdom, and compassion, even an empty cup seems full.

A famous poem by the eleventh-century Japanese poet Izumi Shikibu speaks to this. She wrote:

Although the wind
blows terribly here,
the moonlight also leaks
between the roof planks
of this ruined house.

This is the voice of a woman who has reshaped the container of her life. Most people would choose a house over a view of the moon, but she values the moon more than the house. Because of this, in the absence of material comfort the presence of the moon is enough. She has reshaped the container of her life, and so everything is just enough.

Before kale and quinoa, before blueberries and acai, there was *okara. Okara* — the pulp of soybeans that remains after tofu is made — is a real superfood, or at least it is for monks, nuns, and budget-conscious homemakers. Since it is technically waste or residue, it sells for only $2 or $3 per pound (or is even free) in Asian grocery stores, but it is full of protein and incredibly versatile. It acts as a good meat substitute, or, as in the recipe below, it is gently simmered with vegetables for a soothing and filling side dish. As soon as you buy *okara*, make sure to dry-fry the whole bag until the consistency is like hot sand. This removes unhealthy enzymes and makes it easier to cook with.

At Nisodo, *okara* was part of the go-to breakfast the first day of *sesshin*, or meditation intensive. We would serve it alongside brown-rice porridge. *Sesshin* is silent, and there is very little sensory stimulation, so meals are a big highlight. I still remember the warm, comforting taste of *okara* in the quiet meditation hall.

⬤ SAUTÉED VEGETABLES AND TOFU PULP

Sautéed Vegetables and Tofu Pulp works well for breakfast — it's hot and slightly mushy — but it need not be reserved only for breakfast. *Okara* is also sold in Japanese supermarkets in premade, packaged form.

I remember when I was in charge of making the menu at Nisodo and I wanted to serve *okara*. I asked around about how to obtain it. My friend Hosai-san suggested I go to the local tofu maker and ask if she would give it to us. Sure enough, the tofu maker was more than happy to get the stuff off her hands. Tofu makers produce far more tofu pulp than they can use themselves.

Konnyaku is a gray gelatinous cake made from the corm of a taro-like Asian potato called konjak, or devil's tongue. Widely touted as a health food, it is often thinly sliced in stews and soups. Mirin and sake are two types of rice wine used in Japanese cooking. For shiitake mushrooms, see chapter 3.

For sautéing or pan-frying, peanut and canola oils are fine, but olive oil may muddle the flavors.

Serves 4 to 6 as a side dish

2 dried shiitake mushrooms soaked in 1½ cups water
    at least 4 hours or overnight
2 teaspoons vegetable oil
¾ cup minced carrot (or cut into thin quarter-moons)
3 ounces *konnyaku* (konjak cake), thinly sliced into
    ¾ × ½-inch strips, about ½ cup
2½ cups *okara* (tofu pulp)
1 piece (2 × 2 inches) *abura age* (fried tofu), thinly
    sliced into ¾ × ½-inch strips
3 green onions, thinly sliced, white and green parts
    separated
2 tablespoons plus 1 teaspoon soy sauce
2 tablespoons mirin
2 tablespoons sake
2 teaspoons sugar
Salt and pepper to taste

Remove the shiitakes from the soaking liquid and thinly slice them. Reserve the liquid.

Heat the vegetable oil in a frying pan and sauté the carrot, *konnyaku*, and sliced shiitakes for 2 to 3 minutes, or until the carrot softens. Add the *okara*, *abura age*, and white parts of the green onions. Continue to sauté on medium-low for 3 to 5 minutes, or until the *okara* begins to stick to the bottom of the pan. Add the reserved shiitake liquid, soy sauce, mirin, sake, and sugar. Stir and continue to simmer the *okara* and vegetables until the liquid has mostly evaporated, but the ingredients are not dry. If they begin to dry out, add some more water, soy sauce, and sugar. Stir in the green onion tops and season with salt and pepper to taste.

Meal Ideas: Good at breakfast with rice porridge. Also good at lunch with rice; Miso Soup (p. 54) with yellow onions, Chinese cabbage, and daikon; and Meat 'n' Potatoes for Zen Monks (p. 24).

● MEAT 'N' POTATOES FOR ZEN MONKS
(*NIKU JYAGA FU*)

One wonderful dish that you will rarely, if ever, see at a restaurant is called *niku jyaga*, literally translated "meat (and) potatoes." It's classic Japanese no-frills, no-fuss home cooking, made with beef, potatoes, onions, and carrots in a sweet soy-flavored broth. This dish held a special nostalgic place in the hearts of my Japanese nun friends, so we would often replicate it at the convent using *fu* (high-protein wheat gluten) instead of meat. It's not entirely necessary to add *fu* to this dish, as the potatoes and carrots are hearty enough by themselves. But if you're craving an extra bit of protein, the additional wheat gluten is delicious.

For *konbu* (dried kelp) and dashi (basic Japanese soup stock), see chapter 3.

Serves 4 to 6

> 3 large dried shiitake mushrooms, soaked in 2 cups water overnight
> 1 piece (2 × 2 inches) *konbu* (dried kelp), soaked overnight with the shiitakes, or 1 to 2 teaspoons dashi powder (optional)
> 2 teaspoons vegetable oil
> 1 onion, diced medium
> 2 large potatoes, peeled and cut into bite-size pieces
> 2 carrots, cut into bite-size pieces
> 4 disks (2 inches in diameter) *yaki fu* (dried wheat gluten), about 30 grams (1 ounce)
> Salt to taste

Seasoning for the Potato Mixture
> ¼ cup sake
> 3 tablespoons mirin

1 teaspoon sugar
¼ cup soy sauce

Broth for the *Fu*
1 cup dashi
2 tablespoons mirin
2 tablespoons soy sauce
1 teaspoon sugar
Salt to taste

Remove the shiitakes (and konbu, if using) from the soaking liquid and squeeze them out, reserving the liquid. (Reserve the *konbu* for another use or discard.) Cut the shiitakes into bite-size pieces, either in half or in quarters, depending on their size.

Heat the oil in a large frying pan, wok, or pot. Add the onions and sauté on high for 2 minutes, stirring constantly. Reduce the heat to medium, add the potatoes and carrots, and continue cooking for 3 minutes, until the potatoes begin to turn golden. Add the mushrooms, reserved mushroom liquid, and optional dashi powder and bring to a boil. Lower the heat to medium, cover the vegetables with a lid or durable plate so that they stay submerged under the liquid, and cook until the potatoes are tender, 10 to 15 minutes. Halfway through the cooking time, when the shiitake liquid has reduced a bit, add the sake and mirin. Stir occasionally so that all sides of the potatoes get cooked.

(If the shiitake liquid all boils off during the cooking process, add enough dashi so that the potatoes are at least halfway covered in liquid. If the potatoes still seem dry, add a bit of the broth for the *fu*. It is very important to cook the potatoes all the way through before adding the soy sauce mixture.)

Meanwhile, soak the *fu* in water for about 2 minutes, until it is soft, like a sponge. Drain and squeeze out the water. If necessary, cut the *fu* into bite-size pieces. Combine the ingredients for the *fu* broth (dashi, mirin, soy, sugar, salt) in a saucepan. Add the *fu* and boil gently for 5 minutes, until the *fu* pieces have absorbed the flavor and color of the soy sauce.

Mix together the potato mixture's sugar and soy sauce and add it to the vegetables, a little at a time, until the broth reaches the desired level of sweetness and saltiness. Make sure all the vegetables are coated in sauce and slightly darkened with the soy sauce. Cook for another minute, so that the vegetables can absorb the flavor. When the potatoes and carrots are cooked through and tender, remove the *fu* from its liquid and carefully fold it into the potato mixture. (You will have leftover *fu* broth.) Add salt to taste.

Meal Idea: Serve with rice; Crushed Cucumber and Tomato Salad (p. 26); and Miso Soup (p. 54) with eggplant (cut into bite-size pieces), sliced fresh shiitakes, and green onions.

⦿ CRUSHED CUCUMBER AND TOMATO SALAD

In this recipe, pounding the cucumber helps it absorb the flavor of the dressing. Really, cucumbers can be eaten alone with just salt, but here tomatoes, *shiso*, and ginger are added for a more complex flavor. *Shiso*, a Japanese herb reminiscent of basil, is available in Asian supermarkets.

Serves 2 as a side dish

1 cucumber
2 teaspoons salt
1 large tomato
3 *shiso* leaves
Sesame seeds, for garnish

Dressing
    4 teaspoons soy sauce
    2 teaspoons rice vinegar
    1 teaspoon grated ginger
    Drizzle of sesame oil

Cut the cucumber in half lengthwise and place it in a plastic bag. With a mallet or avocado masher, smash the cucumber until it breaks apart into several pieces and the seeds are completely dislodged. Remove it from the bag and cut it into bite-size pieces. Rub the salt into the cucumber pieces with your hands and place them in a strainer over a bowl. Cover with a plate or other weight and refrigerate for 3 hours.

Immediately before serving, cut the tomato into bite-size pieces. Roll up the *shiso* leaves tightly like cigarettes and slice thinly. Mix the dressing ingredients together in a small bowl. Remove the cucumbers from the refrigerator, squeeze out the excess water, and place them in a bowl. Add the tomatoes, dressing, and sliced *shiso* leaves and gently mix. Garnish with sesame seeds, if desired.

Meal Idea: Serve with rice and Clear Soup (p. 72) with spinach, silken tofu, shimeji mushrooms, and *abura age* or Five-Color Stewed Vegetables (p. 79).

JAPANESE PUMPKIN SALAD

Potato salad with sliced cucumber is a popular dish served throughout Japan and even in Japanese restaurants and markets in the West. At the convent, when putting on a large event or ceremony, we would often make an analogous dish with Japanese pumpkin substituted for potatoes. Garnished with steamed broccoli and a few slices of tomato, pumpkin salad makes a beautiful and filling side dish. It is a little heavy, so it works well paired with a simple, clear soup and an oil-free vegetable or protein dish.

Kabocha, or Japanese pumpkin, is sweeter than Western pumpkin, more similar to a butternut squash. Kabocha is usually eaten with the skin on, as the skin becomes tender enough to eat after cooking. It's up to you whether or not to keep the skin on; while you're cutting up the pumpkin, you'll get a sense of whether the skin seems edible. If there are a lot of warts and blemishes, by all means cut them off, but if the skin is fairly smooth, it's edible. You can also do as professional Japanese chefs do and use a knife to cut off little bits of the skin. Be sure to use kabocha when making this recipe, though. It will not work with a North American pumpkin!

This recipe calls for Japanese mayonnaise, which can be purchased in any Asian grocery. It's inexplicably better than — okay, different from — American mayonnaise, since it is made with apple cider vinegar. Look for Kewpie No Egg Mayonnaise if you want a vegan option.

Serves 3 to 4 as a side dish

> 3 cups (1-inch cubes) kabocha (Japanese pumpkin;
>   from a 2- to 3-pound fruit)
> ½ teaspoon salt
> 1 small cucumber, thinly sliced
> ¾ cup thinly sliced onions
> 2 tablespoons rice vinegar
> Salt and pepper to taste
> ½ cup Japanese mayonnaise

Steam the kabocha cubes for about 15 to 20 minutes, or until the pumpkin is tender and easily pierced with a fork. (If you do not have a steamer, place the pumpkin in a colander inside a pot of boiling water so that the pumpkin is raised above the water and cover the pot with a lid.)

While the pumpkin cooks, stir the ½ teaspoon salt into the cucumbers and let them sit for 15 minutes. Once the cucumbers have absorbed the salt, squeeze them thoroughly to remove excess water, and pat them dry with a towel.

When the pumpkin is tender, remove it from the steamer and place it in a bowl. Immediately add the sliced onions and stir, so that the onions become slightly heated by the steamed pumpkin. (This will work with onions that are fresh and not so bitter. If you are using particularly strong onions, soak them in water and vinegar for 1 hour before use.) Using a masher or a fork, mash the pumpkin until it is soft and the pieces have broken down but are still slightly chunky. Add the vinegar and then a generous amount of salt and pepper. Stir and allow the pumpkin mixture to cool, absorbing the flavor of the onions, vinegar, salt, and pepper.

When the pumpkin has cooled, add the cucumber and mayonnaise. Stir gently to combine. Season with salt and pepper to taste.

Variation: The same ingredients and method can be used with potatoes instead of pumpkin to make potato salad. Substitute 3 cups diced potatoes for the pumpkin, if desired.

Meal Idea: Serve with rice; Simmered Root Vegetables (p. 157) or Five-Color Stewed Vegetables (p. 79); and Miso Soup (p. 54) with tofu, wakame, and green onions.

◉ FRIED JAPANESE PUMPKIN
WITH SWEET VINEGAR

Fried Japanese Pumpkin with Sweet Vinegar is a luxurious sweet-and-sour side dish that is good when paired with something lighter, like simple steamed green beans, carrots, or spinach with a sesame dressing (see Green Beans in Sesame Sauce, p. 148). The way to make this dish delicious is to thinly slice the pumpkin and to be fearless with the sugar in the vinegar. It's not a light dish, but your taste buds will thank you.

Like most of the food in this book, I first ate this fried pumpkin at Nisodo. I remember thinking it was far too decadent for monastery food. Serves me right for assuming anything about Buddhism!

Serves 4 as a side dish

> 1 small kabocha (Japanese pumpkin), sliced into 3 cups
>   of pieces (see below for slicing instructions)
> 1 cup rice vinegar
> ⅓ cup sugar
> 1 teaspoon salt
> 2 tablespoons soy sauce
> Vegetable oil for deep-frying
> ½ onion, sliced lengthwise into ½-inch strips

Carefully cut off a chunk of the pumpkin — depending on your strength, it may be too difficult to cut in half by yourself, so start small, cutting about a third of it and moving on to the rest. With the skin side up, cut the pumpkin piece into very thin (about ¼ inch thick) slices. Then cut the slices in half to create pieces that are about 1 inch wide and 1½ inches long. Cut another chunk of the pumpkin and continue slicing. When finished, you should have about 3 cups of slices.

In a small saucepan, bring the vinegar to a boil. Remove the pan from the heat and stir in the sugar and salt. Stir until the sugar is dissolved, and then add the soy sauce.

Pour at least 1½ inches of oil into a large, deep pan and heat to between 350 and 370°F. (Or if you have a deep-fryer, use it following the manufacturer's directions.) When hot, fry the pumpkin pieces, working in batches, until they are tender and golden brown on the outside, about 1 to 2 minutes. Lift the cooked pumpkin slices out and immediately drop them into the vinegar mixture. Next, fry the onions — they will cook incredibly quickly, so be careful. Lift the onions out and drop them into the vinegar mixture as well.

Allow the vegetables and marinade to cool, flipping the pumpkin pieces once or twice if they are not completely submerged in the vinegar mixture. You can eat this dish once the marinade has cooled and the pumpkin has absorbed the sweet vinegar, or you can refrigerate it and serve it cold.

Meal Idea: Serve with rice, Cold Vegetables with Tofu Dressing (p. 43) or Green Beans in Sesame Sauce (p. 148), and Clear Soup with Bamboo Shoots and Wakame (p. 72).

⬤ TOFU AND WALNUT–STUFFED MUSHROOMS

At the first monastery where I learned to cook temple food, during the fall I would often pop behind the garden wall to pick shiitake mushrooms that grew from a huge old log (see chapter 3 for more on shiitakes). For months this log would produce giant shiitake mushrooms, and it was always a pleasure to grill them and eat them hot, slightly blackened, with just a drizzle of ponzu sauce for flavor. Tofu and Walnut–Stuffed Mushrooms is a slightly more elaborate recipe, adapted from a cookbook in Japanese published by Eiheiji Monastery. The monastery's recipe calls for chestnuts, but since those are hard to find, here I use walnuts.

Makes 10

1 block (14 ounces) firm tofu
10 fresh shiitake mushrooms, the larger the better
1½ teaspoons plus 1 tablespoon vegetable oil, *divided*
¼ cup minced carrot
1 green onion, thinly sliced

Salt
1½ teaspoons soy sauce
¼ cup finely chopped walnuts
4 teaspoons cornstarch, *divided*
Ponzu sauce, for serving

Wrap the tofu in paper towels, cover with a plate or cutting board, put a weight on the plate/board, and let sit for 30 minutes to press out excess water. Place the tofu in a bowl and mash it with a fork. Remove the stems of the mushrooms by pulling and twisting (this will create a larger hole than slicing them off).

In 1½ teaspoons of oil in a small pan, sauté the carrot and green onion together until the carrot is tender, about 2 minutes. Sprinkle with salt and add the soy sauce.

To the tofu in the bowl, add the carrot-onion mixture and chopped walnuts and combine. Sprinkle with salt and mix in 1 teaspoon of the cornstarch. Coat the inside of each mushroom with cornstarch. Roughly divide the tofu mixture into 10 portions and press each together in your hands first to form a small patty. Press the patties into the mushrooms. Spread the rest of the cornstarch on a plate and dip the bottoms (caps) of mushrooms in it so they get coated. Sprinkle any remaining cornstarch over the stuffed tops of the mushrooms.

Heat the remaining 1 tablespoon of oil in a large pan and fry the mushrooms, cap down and stuffing side up, for 2 minutes. Carefully flip the mushrooms over and cook the stuffing side 1 to 2 minutes until golden brown (the top may cook faster than the bottom). When the mushrooms are tender, remove them from heat and place on paper towels to absorb excess oil. Serve hot, with ponzu sauce on the side.

Meal Idea: Serve with rice; Simmered Root Vegetables (p. 157); and Miso Soup (p. 54) with pumpkin, *abura age*, and green onions.

RICE

The Foundation of a Meal

After breakfast, the nuns at Nisodo stand up and bow in unison. The abbess slowly walks out of the dining hall, followed by an eager attendant. As soon as they exit the room, we pour into the kitchen, congratulating the cook on her meal if it was tasty; if it was a terrified novice cooking her first meal, we congratulate her whether it was tasty or not. After a meal is finished there is a great sense of relief among the kitchen group, an impulse to let loose and chat, but after breakfast there is little time to waste. Preparing lunch is the most time-consuming part of the day in the kitchen, and the *tenzo* has only about three hours to cook a meal for thirty or more.

A benefit of *oryoki* meals is that there are fewer dishes to wash. But there are still pots and pans — the pressure cooker used to prepare the rice porridge and the *handai* (bamboo basket) in which the porridge is served. After the meal, the *tenzo* cleans all of these things. She makes sure not to waste a single grain of rice, if possible, even using a special plastic utensil to scrape the inside of the pressure cooker and retrieve bits of browned, sticky rice from the corners. She will put this in a small bowl to eat later and then start lunch preparation. At the end of the *oryoki* ceremony, nuns wash their bowls with hot water and then dump the water into a bamboo bucket. Afterward, the *tenzo* takes this bucket outside and empties it onto the plants. The next thing to do in preparation for lunch is to wash the rice.

It's no exaggeration that you can't say *food* in Japanese without *rice*. The word for "meal" in Japanese, *gohan*, is synonymous with "rice," and the words for "breakfast," "lunch," and "dinner" are "morning rice," "afternoon rice," and "evening rice," respectively. If all the other elements in a meal are on point but the rice is too dry or too wet or hasn't been washed properly, then the whole meal suffers.

The rice used in Japan has grains that are shorter and stickier than their counterparts in the rest of the world; basmati rice, from India, for example, is thinner and longer, and each grain falls away from the others in a bowl. But when using chopsticks to pick up rice, you want the grains to stick together in clumps rather than separate.

In Japan rice is most often served plain, without salt or soy sauce. This is because the other dishes, like miso soup (a soup flavored with fermented soybean paste), fish, and pickles, are usually very salty, and the rice acts as a kind of palate cleanser to balance to the saltiness. Well-washed rice, once cooked, should be shiny and reflect the light. This shininess is achieved by washing the rice thoroughly.

Rice is washed by placing it into a pot or rice cooker and

covering it with water. The rice is swirled around until the water becomes cloudy and then poured into a fine sieve or colander and drained. It is gently scrubbed with the palm of the hand against the sieve for a minute or so. Then it is rinsed with water and returned to the pot. The pot is filled with water again and the procedure is repeated until the water is no longer cloudy but runs clear. This may take several rinses, depending on the age and quality of the rice.

Much of monastic life and many of the regulations in Zen temples are designed to preserve water. In the *Tenzo Kyokun*, Dogen Zenji wrote, "When washing rice, preparing vegetables, and so on, do so with your own hands, with close attention, vigorous exertion, and a sincere mind." He instructs monks to keep the white water rather than discarding it. Rice water is excellent for boiling giant daikon radishes and for treating bamboo to remove the bitterness. Leftover rice water can be poured onto plants.

The nuns at Nisodo taught me to let the washed rice sit for twenty minutes in the sieve before putting it in water again. This allows oxygen to enter the rice, making the rice more airy and preventing clumps. After airing for twenty minutes, the nuns would then soak the rice in water for at least an hour, if not more, before beginning to cook it. This allows the rice to absorb enough water to be soft and moist.

Although a pressure cooker is useful for making rice porridge, an electric rice cooker is the ideal way to make regular white rice. Using an electric rice cooker removes the uncertainty of having to figure out how much water to use and how long to cook the rice, and there is no decrease in quality (in fact, it tastes better in my opinion). You simply put the rice in, fill the cooker with water to the desired mark, and press "Start."

If you don't have a rice cooker, your cooking time and water-to-rice ratio will vary depending on the kind of rice.

Luckily, packages of rice almost always list cooking time and instructions. For example, the rice I currently cook with suggests bringing 2 cups of water and 1½ cups rice to a boil in a covered saucepan and simmering for 20 minutes.

Rice can be a standalone dish. In the same way that good bread, with a drizzle of olive oil, salt, and pepper, can be a meal in itself, good rice, when properly prepared, is sufficient alone or with a sprinkling of *furikake*, salty seaweed seasoning. Rice is the first thing a monastery cook attends to in the morning and the last thing she attends to at night, when she washes and prepares the rice for the next morning's porridge.

At Nisodo, lunch was the most elaborate meal of the day. In addition to rice, soup, and a vegetable, we would also be served a side dish (or two!) called *ippan*, which literally means "one dish." Because *ippan* are plated separately, they could be cooked with oil, unlike the soup and vegetable dishes spooned into the *oryoki* bowls. As *ippan* the *tenzo* could slip fun, oily, or Western dishes into the meal. What I discovered in my years at Nisodo is that nuns are excellent at bending rules in such a way that the rules stay intact. For example, sometimes we would use only the middle *oryoki* bowl for a consommé soup and be served an "*ippan*" of spaghetti with red sauce or even a sandwich to go with it. In this way, we were able to rationalize bypassing the traditional *oryoki* custom to incorporate more diverse tastes. *Ippan* could also be complicated rice dishes: fried rice or colorful sushi rice made to resemble the fishy kind sold in restaurants.

After lunch, if we were lucky, we could take a few minutes of rest. Napping while lying down was not allowed, so we all became skilled at napping while sitting up or napping with our heads on our desks. But there was no rest for the *tenzo*. After lunch, of course, comes dinner. The *tenzo* is usually the first person to begin work and the last person to finish. After dinner, she may receive help in cleaning up the kitchen, but she may not. If something went wrong with the meal, she would undoubtedly hear about it, but if everything went off without a hitch, she might not receive a word of thanks or praise.

Aoyama Roshi, the abbess of Nisodo, was fond of saying that the *tenzo* is the "hidden power beneath the floorboards," a common Japanese idiom to describe people who are influential without being seen. Becoming accustomed to this kind of hard, hidden work (metaphorically under the floorboards) is useful. Our work needs to matter for the activity, intention, and effort itself, not only for the praise we receive. Praise and blame come and go, so we need to develop some kind of internal compass that guides us through the world when there are no external signposts.

After I published my first book, I became frustrated with what I perceived to be a lack of recognition. When I could remind myself that I wrote the book not for fame but to help young women going through hard times as I had, my suffering dissipated (and in fact, my book did quite well — it was just my critical mind that invented a reality in which I had failed). Working hard for others and being unattached to the outcome is a muscle we strengthen every time we take up the pen, keyboard, stethoscope, or the spatula. Every time we engage with a pure intention, with our whole body and mind, it becomes easier to do it again and be pleased with the outcome, whatever it is.

● COLORFUL "SUSHI" RICE

Sushi chirashi, or "mixed sushi rice," is a high-class specialty served in sushi restaurants in Japan. This dish is usually comprised of a bowl full of sweet vinegared rice covered in a layer of assorted sashimi (raw fish), fish eggs, and shredded egg. The vegan version of this begins with the same vinegared rice, but layers on edamame (green soybeans), stewed shiitakes (see chapter 3), *koyadofu* (tofu), grated carrot, and avocado. This provides a variety of interesting textures and plenty of umami (see chapter 3). In Japan, hardly anyone eats avocado with rice — this is a California innovation — but I do enjoy the rich fattiness of avocado.

Koyadofu is a kind of freeze-dried tofu that is reconstituted in water and then stewed so that it absorbs the flavor of the broth. It has a spongy texture that is off-putting to some Westerners. If you can't find *koyadofu* in an Asian market or if the notion of a "spongy" texture doesn't appeal to you, you can of course substitute sliced grilled tofu. But I think the inclusion of *koyadofu* helps approximate the taste and texture of raw fish.

Edamame can be purchased already shelled, which is easiest, or you can boil the unshelled beans for 5 minutes, drain, rinse, and then squeeze out the beans.

I first ate this dish at Nisodo. We were required to use the formal black lacquered *oryoki* bowls at all three meals, but if the cook wanted to serve an *ippan*, a separately plated specialty dish like this recipe, she would do away with the large rice bowl. We would eat soup from our middle bowl, the *ippan*, and pickles, of course.

Serves 2

1 piece (2 × 2 inches) *konbu* (dried kelp)
2 cups uncooked rice
5 tablespoons sushi vinegar or 2 tablespoons sugar
        dissolved in 5 tablespoons rice vinegar
1 block (about ½ ounce) *koyadofu* (freeze-dried tofu)
4 small dried shiitake mushrooms or 2 larger ones cut
        in half, soaked overnight in enough water to cover
1 cup cooked and shelled edamame (green soybeans)
1 carrot, julienned or grated

1 avocado, sliced
Sesame seeds, for garnish
Shredded nori, for garnish (optional)

Broth for the *Koyadofu*
1 cup dashi
1 tablespoon soy sauce
1½ teaspoons sugar
1½ teaspoons sake
1½ teaspoons mirin

Broth for the Shiitakes
½ cup dashi
1 tablespoon sugar
1 tablespoon soy sauce

Add *konbu* to the rice and cook the rice according to package directions. When the rice is done, remove the *konbu*. Pour the rice into a bamboo serving basket or a heat-resistant bowl. Drizzle the vinegar over the hot rice and mix vigorously with a rice paddle. As you mix in the vinegar, fan the rice with a paper fan. This allows the rice to cool faster and makes it shiny rather than dull.

Reconstitute the *koyadofu* by soaking it in water for 5 minutes. After it has expanded and become soft, remove it from the water and squeeze out the excess liquid. Bring the dashi, soy sauce, sugar, sake, and mirin to a boil in a saucepan. Add the *koyadofu* and simmer for 10 minutes. Remove the pan from the heat and allow the liquid to cool completely, if time allows. This will allow the *koyadofu* to absorb even more of the flavor from the broth.

Remove the shiitakes from the soaking liquid and slice them very thinly. In a saucepan bring the dashi, sugar, and soy sauce to a boil and add the shiitakes. Cook on medium for

5 minutes or until the mushrooms are cooked through. Be careful — the broth is very sweet and may caramelize and burn!

Once the *koyadofu* has cooled, remove it from the broth, cut it in half lengthwise, and then slice it into ⅛-inch slices.

Spread the rice onto two plates in even layers. Keeping each ingredient separate, arrange the *koyadofu*, sliced shiitakes, edamame, and carrot on top of the rice, half on each plate. Layer the avocado slices carefully over everything. Garnish with sesame seeds and/or nori.

Meal Idea: This dish is a meal in itself. All it needs is a soup, like Clear Soup (p. 72) with sliced green beans, wakame, and green onions.

The daikon, or giant radish, is one of my favorite Japanese vegetables. In its raw form, it's actually quite bitter. It's not fancy, sweet, or even all that interesting — one could say it is the ultimate Zen vegetable.

A dish called Daikon "Steak" is seared into my memory, because it was the first dish I was ever required to prepare when it was my turn to be cook for the day at Nisodo. I remember that the menu maker, who was in charge of making sure everything got on the table on time, was strict and very scary. I had three hours to prepare rice, soup, a side dish, and this daikon and miso sauce for about thirty people. Because I was so inexperienced in the kitchen, I spent about an hour and a half just cutting up and cooking the daikon! The menu maker came in to check on me, and her eyes bulged at my lack of progress. She yelled at me and then took over the side dish, so that we could serve lunch on time.

Years later, when I was comfortable cooking Japanese food and had a turn at being the menu maker myself, it was my job to cook pork dumplings wrapped in thinly sliced daikon.

This involved slicing the radish with a mandolin, sealing the dumplings with a toothpick, and then frying them. It was a challenging meal that could have flopped, but I prepared it correctly with time to spare. This was evidence to me of how far I'd come as a chef. Now I realize that Daikon "Steak" is actually an easy beginners' dish, which is probably why it was assigned to me on my first day!

⬤ DAIKON "STEAK"

For Daikon "Steak," we boil the daikon twice: first in leftover rice water, which removes the bitterness, and then in *konbu* broth, which allows the daikon to absorb the flavor of seaweed ever so slightly. Next, the daikon is coated and fried in hot oil until golden brown and crispy; then it is topped with a tangy, salty miso sauce (*dengaku*). It is perfect for a cold winter day when paired with rice and clear soup.

Having a great miso sauce (*dengaku*) really makes this dish. If you can't find any at a local Japanese market, you can make the sauce yourself (recipe below).

Serves 6

> 1 piece (5 × 7 inches) *konbu* (dried kelp)
> 1 quart water
> 1 daikon, 6 inches long
> Leftover water from washing rice (enough to cover daikon)
> *Katakuriko* (potato starch) or regular cornstarch
> 1 tablespoon vegetable oil, or more, for frying
> Yuzu *dengaku* sauce (yuzu-flavored miso sauce; store-bought or made from the recipe below), for serving

Julienned yuzu (Japanese lemon) or lemon peel,
for garnish

Soak the *konbu* in the water in a large pot for at least 1 hour.

Cut the daikon horizontally into 1-inch disks, so you have 6 disks. Peel the daikon by cutting off the outer ⅛ inch of skin (use a knife — a peeler won't get deep enough, but save the leftover skin for a stir-fry; see chapter 11). With a sharp knife, make four ½-inch slits in the center of each daikon disk.

Place the daikon disks into a pot of leftover rice water, bring to a boil, and cook for 15 minutes. Drain the disks and add them to the pot with the *konbu* and water. Bring to a boil and cook for another 10 to 15 minutes, or until completely tender. Drain the disks and pat them dry with a towel.

Coat each side of the daikon disks with *katakuriko* or cornstarch. Heat the oil in a frying pan on medium-high. Add the daikon disks and pan-fry them 3 to 4 minutes on one side. Flip and cook the other side until golden brown, 3 to 4 minutes. Remove the disks from the pan and place them on a tray lined with paper towels to absorb excess oil.

If desired, cut the leftover *konbu* into 1-inch-square pieces and fry them in leftover oil until slightly crispy. Arrange the fried *konbu* on a plate and place one daikon disk on each square of *konbu* (you may have leftover *konbu*). Top each disk with 1 tablespoon of *dengaku* sauce and garnish with julienned yuzu peel.

Yuzu-Flavored Miso Sauce (Yuzu *Dengaku*)
    4 tablespoons miso paste
    4 tablespoons sugar
    4 tablespoons mirin
    Peel of ½ yuzu (Japanese lemon), julienned

Heat a frying pan on medium-high. Add the miso, sugar, mirin, and the yuzu peel. Mix with a spatula or wooden spoon to combine. When the sauce starts to boil, reduce the heat and simmer, stirring frequently, until the sauce has reduced, about 5 minutes.

Meal Idea: Serve with rice, Green Beans in Sesame Sauce (p. 148), and Clear Soup (p. 72) with *fu* and *mitsuba*.

● COLD VEGETABLES WITH TOFU DRESSING (*SHIRAE*)

Shirae is one of my favorite dishes — a sweet, filling, delicate dish with no oil that is a great way to eat both vegetables and protein. The word *shirae* combines the characters for "white" and "mix," because tofu is the main ingredient and everything is mixed together. Essentially you will make a combination of cooked vegetables, season them with soy sauce, and then toss them in a thick tofu and sesame dressing ("dressing" is perhaps the wrong word — the tofu mixture is a major part of the dish, not an incidental add-on).

Although this recipe uses carrots and spinach, other vegetables can be substituted for the spinach, such as green beans, broccoli, or asparagus.

Serves 4 as a side dish

8 ounces firm tofu
3 ounces *konnyaku* (konjak cake), cut into thin
    1 × ½-inch slices
½ cup thinly sliced carrot (1 × ½-inch slices)
2 cups dashi
2 tablespoons soy sauce

1 tablespoon sugar
2 tablespoons sake
½ cup cooked and chopped spinach
Salt to taste

Seasoning for the Dressing

2 tablespoons sesame seeds
2 tablespoons mirin
1 tablespoon soy sauce
2 tablespoons strong dashi

Wrap the tofu in paper towels, top with a plate or cutting board, put a weight on top, and let sit to press out the water for about 30 minutes.

Bring a small saucepan of water to a boil, add the *konnyaku*, and cook for 4 minutes. Add the carrots and cook for 1 minute. Drain and rinse with cool water.

Mix the dashi, soy sauce, sugar, and sake in a medium saucepan and bring to a boil. Add the *konnyaku* and carrot, and simmer for 10 minutes. Remove the pan from the heat and add the cooked and chopped spinach. Let cool for 5 minutes; as the mixture cools, the vegetables will absorb the flavor. Drain all the vegetables (save the broth for soup, if you like) and cool them completely. Squeeze out excess moisture with a cloth.

Toast the sesame seeds in a small dry pan on low heat for 2 to 5 minutes, watching carefully so they don't burn. Grind them using a small food processor, a mortar and pestle, or a traditional Japanese sesame seed grinder (*suribachi*).

In a small bowl mix together the sesame seeds, mirin, soy sauce, and dashi. In a large bowl, using an avocado masher or pestle, mash the tofu until it is smooth. Add the sesame mixture and stir to combine.

Add the cooled vegetables to the tofu dressing. With your hands, mix the vegetables into the tofu, making sure they are evenly distributed. Add salt to taste.

Meal Idea: Serve with rice; Marinated Fried Eggplant (p. 95); and Miso Soup (p. 54) with potatoes, yellow onions, and carrots.

3

BROTH

How to Enhance
Your Surroundings

Good dashi, or Japanese umami stock, is like a good Zen practice. We should never notice it is there, but we should miss it if it's gone. Good stock flavors the whole dish. It gives the food that something special, that extra deliciousness, but it's almost an afterthought. If you taste the dashi explicitly in food, it's too strong. Soup and vegetable dishes should not taste like seaweed and shiitake mushrooms per se. They should taste like themselves. Dashi helps food taste more like itself. Zen practice helps us be more of ourselves. If your Zen practice is more obvious and apparent than your personality, then something is amiss. It should be in the background, making your life taste delicious.

The umami in dashi is what makes the soup and other

dishes create a subtle and pleasant buzz, or "furriness," in your mouth. *Umami*, once a relatively unknown Japanese term, has entered the cultural vocabulary lately, even finding its way into the name of the popular Los Angeles burger joint Umami Burger, which serves "umamified" fries in truffle oil. During the last few decades, scientists have recognized umami as an official taste, joining the well-known basic tastes of sweet, sour, bitter, and salty. The umami flavor is caused by the glutamate in fish and seaweed, an amino acid crucial in the formation of protein. MSG, or monosodium glutamate, is an isolated form of the glutamate responsible for producing the umami "taste." MSG is odorless, colorless, and tasteless, but it increases the overall savory quality of food.

As a child, I always enjoyed MSG-heavy Chinese food (much to the horror of my health-conscious, crunchy parents), so I was pleasantly surprised to learn during my time in Japan that MSG occurs naturally in umami stock made from seaweed (MSG is the white powder on the outside of kelp, so make sure not to wash kelp before you use it for stock). Umami also exists in mushrooms, especially shiitake mushrooms, and in fermented foods like soy sauce, nutritional yeast, and cheese.

MSG is not bad for you. In fact, as Caitlin Dewey noted recently in the *Washington Post*, the fear of MSG health risks stems from one letter written to the *New England Journal of Medicine* — rather than a body of peer-reviewed research — in 1968. In the letter, health researcher Ho Man Kwow claimed to have become sick after eating at a Chinese restaurant, leading to the term "Chinese restaurant syndrome." After this letter, several people wrote to the journal detailing their own sicknesses after eating at Chinese restaurants, and an anecdotal health crisis was born.

Yet the links between MSG and sickness are not backed up by science. MSG is simply an amino acid, and researchers now believe the myth of MSG health risks persists because of anti-Asian bias as well as other factors associated with eating at Chinese restaurants, such as excess alcohol and salt consumption. Researchers also note that our culture has become one in which people are more likely to believe personal, anecdotal accounts rather than scientific facts, and there is never a shortage of people claiming to have become sick from MSG.

Because of all of these factors, our collective fear of MSG has persisted. MSG also occurs in things like tomatoes, cheese, Doritos, and — as I mentioned in the case of Umami Burger — truffle oil, and yet people rarely, if ever, complain about sickness from these types of foods. Apparently it is only the MSG in food from Asian restaurants that seems to produce illness.

"What causes Chinese restaurant syndrome?" Anthony Bourdain asked rhetorically on his TV show *Parts Unknown*. He answered his own question: "Racism."

This is good news for us, because good stock — which contains MSG — is crucial to Japanese cooking (and if you are still convinced MSG gives you a headache, there are ways to make dashi without MSG). It of course makes the base for miso soup and noodle broth, but it also is the background for the sauces in stir-fries, stews, and even salads. If your stock is weak, the whole dish will taste uninteresting and lifeless.

Usually, soup stock in Japan is made with bonito flakes, and recreating the same sensation for vegetarians is somewhat tricky. The traditional vegetarian Buddhist way of creating stock is to make it with *konbu* and shiitake mushrooms. *Konbu* is dried edible kelp used especially for flavoring stock. It also can be soaked overnight in water and is wrapped around salmon or daikon as a traditional New Year's delicacy called *konbu maki*. *Konbu* comes in many shapes and sizes — from yard-long unpackaged strips to smaller precut pieces — but you will recognize it by its dark, almost blackish green color and leathery appearance. The edges of *konbu* can be crinkled, like a pie crust, or the whole sheet can be smooth and symmetrical, cut into a neat square.

Shiitakes are a kind of Japanese mushroom that is particularly savory (i.e., filled with umami). They have brown caps and white stalks, and in their fresh state they can be as large in diameter as a softball. At Toshoji, the monastery where I was ordained, there was a log in a dried-out creek bed behind the vegetable garden that would be covered with shiitakes every autumn. It was a joy to trudge back to the hidden, insect-swarming place in the forest with a bowl and pick shiitakes easily off of the log, my boots crunching over the fallen yellow leaves. Drying magnifies the flavor and savoriness of fresh shiitakes. Dried shiitakes are slightly darker than the fresh kind, hard, and need to be reconstituted in water. These are usually sold in Asian supermarkets in the same aisle as dried *konbu*, since they are both used for stock.

◉ DASHI

Traditional dashi is made from dried shiitake mushrooms and *konbu*. If you are not used to the taste of shiitake mushrooms, this style of stock can be a little overwhelming. To temper the strong taste of shiitake mushrooms, soybean stock can be added.

Makes 1 quart

> 3 to 6 dried shiitake mushrooms, about ¾ cup
> 1 piece (5 × 6 inches) *konbu* (dried kelp)
> 1 quart water
> 2 ounces dried soybeans (optional)
> 2 cups water (optional)

Add the dried shiitakes and *konbu* to the quart of water in a medium pot and let them soak for at least 5 hours. On low, start heating the stock. Just before it boils remove the *konbu* and shiitakes and then take the pot off the heat. Do not simmer the *konbu* or shiitakes (if using shiitakes in cooking, they will need to be boiled longer, but boiling them here will make the stock too strong).

If desired, toast the soybeans in a dry pan until their aroma emerges, about 4 minutes, stirring constantly so they don't burn. Bring 2 cups of water to a boil in a saucepan, add the soybeans, and remove the pan from the heat. Soak the toasted soybeans in the water for 12 hours. This stock can be used to dilute the shiitake-and-*konbu* dashi to taste (it can also be used by itself for other dishes).

Variation: To make *konbu* dashi, simply omit the shiitakes and soybean stock above. *Konbu* dashi is favored for use in certain dishes, like *sumashi*, Clear Soup (p. 72).

Another option is to use premade dashi powder (add 1 to 2 teaspoons to 3 cups of hot water) or dashi packets (simmer 1 packet in 2 cups of water for 5 minutes). Vegetarian (seaweed or mushroom) dashi powder can be purchased in most Asian markets or online (search "dashi no moto" and look for the green packages with the word *konbu* in the title).

This is the easiest option, favored by house cooks all over Japan, and I am not so much of a purist that I think using them is somehow inauthentic (in fact, it is probably more common in Japanese culture to use instant powder than make dashi from scratch). You will reliably get good-tasting stock this way, without the work of soaking, cooking, and storing the stock. MSG-free options are available, such as Kayanoya Dashi, if the above passionate defense of MSG has not convinced you!

A famous sutra chanted every day in Zen monasteries in Japan is called the *Hokyo Zanmai*, or "Song of the Precious Mirror

Samadhi." Although it is popular today in Japan, it was originally written in ninth-century China as a poem by a monk named Tozan Ryokai (Dongshan Liangjie in Chinese). The final lines of the poem read, "Practice in secret, like a fool, like an idiot. Just to continue in this way is called the host within the host."

This attitude is very important in Zen practice. We do not practice Buddhism to show off or to gain approval from others, and we don't sit in meditation to have cool-looking photos for Instagram. It's really a secret practice, in the sense that you shouldn't need to publicize or show it off. Because you are the only person who can live your life, the focus should be on yourself, on living a good life with your whole body and mind.

We need to devote considerable energy to Buddhist practice, and yet if we are doing it right, our practice should be imperceptible to others. Sometimes in Japan you hear the phrase "the stink of Zen." This is used to describe people who become obsessed with showing off their Zen practice or whose practice is very loud and obvious to others. Ideally, our practice should make us get along better with others, but the obvious thing should be our kind and peaceful demeanor, for example, not the practice itself.

When I was first starting out as a nun in Japan, I took everything very literally and very seriously. This was both good and bad, because although I was trying hard, I was also acting very intensely and competitively. I wanted to follow all the rules and learn all the ceremonies perfectly so that people would respect me. I think because I was one of the only foreigners at the monastery, I felt pressure to be perfect and prove that foreigners could be good Zen monks. I practiced very seriously, but I also alienated people because I got angry easily and didn't understand how to let go.

Over and over, my teachers instructed me to have "secret practice," to practice like water. Water is strong but has no fixed shape; it can move into any container. When you are living with others in a monastery, it is more important to focus on having good practice for yourself and on being part of the team, not on being the best in order to distinguish yourself from everyone else.

This is why we are instructed to "practice in secret, like a fool, like an idiot." This runs counter to the cultural narrative that says that to be successful, we need external recognition. On the contrary, Zen practice is about finding a firm, solid, upright way of living that doesn't depend on external circumstances or other people. The most respected people in a monastery or in an organization are often the quietest ones who work the hardest. They are respected because they work hard not for recognition, but for the work itself. Other people can see this.

Another way of articulating "the stink of Zen" is the Japanese proverb *Miso no miso kusaki wa jyo miso ni arazu,* or "Miso that smells like miso is not good miso." Miso is of course salty fermented soybean paste that is mixed into hot water to make miso soup. The soup's taste is quite distinctive, but miso soup shouldn't smell like anything other than the vegetables in it. If your miso paste smells like anything, it's gone bad. This is a good lesson for anything in life, whether it is a career, love, or a spiritual practice. Our life is functioning its best when things are just as they are — nothing overly exaggerated.

It is important not to boil miso soup after adding miso. This will change the flavor. Make your soup, turn off the heat, and then add miso. Do your best, and walk away. I believe this is the ultimate goal of spiritual practice; we should be like a water wheel that is in just enough water to turn, but not so much that the wheel can't move. This practice of skillful action helps us engage better in politics and in our relationships. Whether in politics or in love, we need to learn how to engage just enough: to give our all, then walk away, and let the flavors settle.

● MISO SOUP

Serves 4 to 6

> 4 cups dashi
> ¼ cup thinly sliced carrots
> 1 cup cubed silken tofu
> 3 to 5 heaping tablespoons miso paste
> ¼ cup sliced green onions, for garnish

Bring the dashi to a boil in a soup pot. Add the carrots and simmer for 2 minutes, or until tender. Add the tofu, which will sink to the bottom. Simmer until the tofu floats. Turn off the heat. Add 3 heaping tablespoons of miso to a miso strainer (a special tool used to dissolve miso in hot broth) and then place this into the soup. Use a spoon or chopsticks to muddle the paste into the hot dashi.

Taste the soup. Depending on the miso you are using, you may need to add another 1 to 2 tablespoons. I like Momofuku chef David Chang's suggestion for how much salt to use in a dish (miso contains a large amount of salt): make food that's "not too salty but almost" too salty. In other words, make miso soup that almost has too much miso. At the very end, garnish with green onions.

Variations: As above, cook all your vegetables in stock until they are tender, turn off the heat, and then add the miso at the very end, followed by any garnish:

- Sliced yellow onions, cubed kabocha (Japanese pumpkin), and sliced *abura age* (fried tofu)
- Cubed tofu and wakame (seaweed), garnished with green onions

- Eggplant (cut into bite-size pieces) and sliced fresh shiitake mushrooms, garnished with green onions
- Cut-up potatoes, carrots, and yellow onions
- Thinly sliced daikon and cubed kabocha, garnished with green onions
- Sliced *abura age* and spinach (or *komatsuna*), garnished with green onions
- Sliced *abura age*, spinach, and sliced yellow onions
- Snap peas (thinly sliced on the diagonal), baby bamboo, and wakame, garnished with green onions

The monastery where I was ordained was over a thousand years old. The wooden pillars were faded, and there was a hole in the Buddha hall that looked straight through to the ground. Many of the doors and windows were made of paper, according to Japanese tradition. In the winter, the cold seeped through the monastery's feeble walls, and I could see my breath in the morning as I chanted. The coldest I have ever been in my life was the first winter I spent in Japan. Every day we would make a point of checking the thermometer in the Buddha hall; if it was above freezing, that was a warm day.

In frigid temperatures like this, hot food was a blessing. One of my favorite winter foods was *kenchin jiru*.

● HEARTY COUNTRY STEW (*KENCHIN JIRU*)

Kenchin jiru is a hearty country-style stew lightly flavored with miso. The more vegetables in this, the better. It should be thick and filling. To shave the gobo, imagine you're sharpening a pencil the old-fashioned way: hold the root in one hand and use a knife to flick flakes off the point with the other. Cutting it this way and then soaking it allows it to become soft and tender in the stew.

Serves 4

> 1 cup shaved *gobo* (burdock root)
> 8 ounces firm tofu
> 2 dried shiitake mushrooms soaked overnight in
>   2 cups water
> 1 piece (2 × 4 inches) *konbu* (dried kelp) soaked
>   1 to 4 hours or overnight in 2 cups water
> 2 teaspoons sesame oil
> ½ cup thinly sliced *konnyaku* (konjak cake; 1 × ½-inch
>   strips)
> 1 cup thinly sliced carrot (in quarter-moons or strips)
> 1 cup thinly sliced daikon (in quarter-moons)
> 1 tablespoon sake
> 1 teaspoon dashi powder (optional)
> 2 tablespoons mirin
> 2 teaspoons sugar
> 1 tablespoon soy sauce
> 1 bunch (4 to 7 ounces) enoki or shimeji mushrooms,
>   separated, cut into 1-inch pieces
> 1 heaping tablespoon miso paste
> 2 green onions, sliced, for garnish

Soak the *gobo* shavings in water for 1 hour and then drain.

Wrap the tofu in paper towels, cover with a plate or cutting board, put a weight on the plate/board, and let sit for 30 minutes to press out excess water.

Remove the shiitakes from the soaking liquid, squeeze out the excess, and thinly slice the mushrooms. Reserve the soaking liquid. Remove the *konbu* from its soaking liquid and discard or save for another use (you may want to use the *konbu* in another dish, or even in this one, if you like the taste of kelp). Reserve the *konbu* soaking liquid.

Heat the sesame oil in a soup pot or deep skillet. Add the

konnyaku and stir-fry it for 2 minutes. Next add the *gobo*, carrot, daikon, and sliced shiitakes, and sauté for another 2 minutes, until the daikon is just beginning to brown. Add the sake, stir, and let it cook off.

After the sake has cooked off, add the shiitake and *konbu* soaking liquids. (For more flavor add the dashi powder as well, if desired.) Bring to a boil, and then add the mirin, sugar, and soy sauce. Simmer the vegetables until tender.

While the vegetables simmer, unwrap the tofu and, using your hands, crumble it into little pieces. In a separate frying pan, dry-fry the tofu (or add a few drops of sesame oil to the pan) until it begins to jump out of the pan and is starting to turn golden. Add the cooked tofu to the stew. Add the enoki mushrooms as well, and cook for 1 minute until the mushrooms are tender.

Bring everything to a boil one last time and then remove the pan from the heat. Dissolve the miso paste into the stew using a miso strainer if you have one. Garnish with the green onions.

Meal Idea: Serve with white rice, Meat 'n' Potatoes for Zen Monks (p. 24), and Julienned Daikon and Carrot in Sweet Vinegar Sauce (p. 156).

● FRIED TOFU IN SAUCE (TOFU *AGEDASHI*)

A necessary component in Fried Tofu in Sauce is excellent dashi, which in turn makes excellent sauce. Similar to Marinated Fried Eggplant (p. 95), this dish involves deep-frying tofu and serving it in a strong sweet-and-salty broth garnished with grated daikon and ginger. The grated ginger blends into the broth and gives the simple tofu a rich and satisfying flavor.

I know I say this about everything, but this truly is one of my all-time favorite Japanese foods. We would prepare this on special occasions at Nisodo, for example, for the annual ceremony to honor the temple members' ancestors. For this event, the people would come to take part in the ceremonies and then dine in a private area afterward.

For this meal we would take out the formal *obon*, or black lacquered serving trays that you often see in fancy restaurants in Kyoto. We would spend days cleaning, prepping vegetables, and choosing and setting out the dishes. For the kitchen work group this was a particularly stressful time, because we had to serve about eight specialty dishes to order, as in a restaurant, rather than follow our staple rice, soup, and side-dish routine. Invariably, one of the eight dishes was either this Fried Tofu in Sauce or Marinated Fried Eggplant. Whoever was in charge of running the frying station would be covered in sweat by the end of the day, but the meal break when we could sample the specialty dishes was always a highlight.

Tofu *agedashi* is served in restaurants and *izakaya* bars (pubs) throughout Japan. In the United States, it has made its way to *izakaya* in major cities, but I'm always disappointed in the way it tastes. A gauge for the quality of an American Japanese restaurant is how well it prepares tofu *agedashi*. It's not a hard dish to make, but something is often lost in translation. In this recipe, I cut a block of tofu into thirds because this is how we would celebrate and honor our guests (by giving them big pieces!), but you can cut the tofu into smaller pieces, as they do in *izakaya*, if you prefer.

Serves 3

1 block (14 to 16 ounces) firm tofu
½ cup cornstarch or *katakuriko* (potato starch)
Vegetable oil for deep-frying
½ cup grated daikon, for garnish

4 teaspoons grated ginger, for garnish
1 green onion, thinly sliced, for garnish

Sauce
1 cup dashi
1 tablespoon sugar
1 tablespoon mirin
3 tablespoons soy sauce

Cut the tofu into thirds and wrap each piece in paper towels. Cover all three with a tray or cutting board, put a weight on the tray/board, and let sit for 30 minutes to press out excess water. Remove the towels. If you prefer smaller pieces, cut the tofu into 1½-inch cubes. Pat the tofu dry with towels.

Bring the dashi, sugar, mirin, and soy sauce to a boil in a small saucepan. Simmer for 2 minutes, stir, and turn off the heat. Cover the saucepan with a lid.

On a plate or cutting board, spread the cornstarch or *katakuriko* into an even layer. Dip the tofu pieces in the starch, coating them evenly. Shake off any excess starch and set aside.

Pour at least 1½ inches of oil into a large deep pan and heat to between 350 and 370°F. (Or if you have a deep-fryer, use it following the manufacturer's directions.) Working in batches, drop the tofu into the oil and fry until golden brown, flipping once. Remove the tofu from the oil and place it briefly on paper towels to absorb excess oil.

Divide the tofu among three small bowls. Spoon the hot soy broth over the tofu and garnish with the grated daikon, ginger, and sliced onions. Serve immediately, while the tofu is still hot.

Meal Ideas: Serve with rice; Miso Soup (p. 54) with daikon, pumpkin, and green onions; and Julienned Daikon and Carrot in Sweet Vinegar Sauce (p. 156) or a salad with Asian dressing. Or make it a happy-hour snack with boiled, salted edamame and beer.

● WINTER HOT POT (*SUKIYAKI NABE*)

Behold, the hot pot! Beloved wintertime meal, maker of memories with your family around a warm *kotasu* (heated table), and excuse to drink copious amounts of sake. *Sukiyaki* is one of many hot pot–style dishes popular throughout Japan (*suki* means "like," *yaki* means "cooked," and *nabe* means "pot," so *sukiyaki* literally means a hot pot full of things you like). It is a classic winter dish, hot and filling — it's a meal in itself, really, since it is usually cooked with a variety of vegetables, tofu, and beef and served piping hot at the table with raw egg to dip the meat into.

The feeling of *sukiyaki nabe* is warm and communal, because families (read: mothers) will often make this dish in an electric hot pot in the center of the table, from which family members remove ingredients as soon as the meat is cooked. I think the same warm, satisfying feeling can be replicated with tofu, *fu* (wheat gluten), the right stock, and a good group of friends and family to share the meal with.

Serves 4

1 package (8 ounces) *shirataki* (*konnyaku* noodles)
1 teaspoon salt
½ medium Chinese (napa) cabbage
1 bunch (4 to 7 ounces) enoki or shimeji mushrooms
6 fresh shiitake mushrooms
2 thick green onions
½ cup *komachibu fu* (small dried gluten), or other *fu*,
    in bite-size pieces
1 block (14 to 16 ounces) broiled or seared tofu,
    cut into 1-inch cubes
½ carrot, julienned

Broth
 1 cup strong dashi (such as shiitake)
 ⅓ cup mirin
 ⅓ cup sake
 ⅓ cup soy sauce
 1 tablespoon sugar
 Salt to taste

Cook the noodles. Drain the *shirataki* noodles and rinse well. Sprinkle with salt, let sit for 10 minutes, and then rinse off the salt.

Break the cabbage leaves apart. Separate the white and green parts of the leaves by cutting the green parts into bite-size pieces and the white parts into smaller pieces.

Cut the bottom inch off of the enoki or shimeji mushrooms and separate them into inch-thick bundles (they are likely to shrink and fall apart as they cook). Remove the stems of the shiitake mushrooms and cut two slits on the top of each mushroom to form an *X*. Cut the green onions on the diagonal into ¼-inch pieces. Separate the white and green parts.

Soak the *fu* in water briefly, for about 2 minutes, until it is soft. Remove and squeeze out the water.

In a large pot, bring all the broth ingredients to a boil, then lower the heat to medium, and cook for 1 minute. Add the *fu*, tofu, shiitakes, and the white parts of the cabbage and green onions (if you are using a hot pot at the table, sauté these ingredients before adding the broth). As you are adding the ingredients, keep them separated in distinct places and do not stir the pot. Cook the vegetables, tofu, and *fu* for 5 minutes, and then add the enoki mushrooms, *shirataki*, green parts of the cabbage, and julienned carrots. Cook for another 4 to 5 minutes, until vegetables are tender and tofu and *fu* have absorbed the flavor of the broth. At the last minute, add the green parts of the green onions.

Divide the vegetables and tofu equally into four bowls, keeping the ingredients as separate as possible. Spoon a liberal amount of broth over the vegetables. If you are using a hot pot at the table, allow guests to serve themselves.

4

BAMBOO

Or, How to Turn Poison into a Meal

If there is a better metaphor for Buddhist practice than turning inedible vegetables into delicious food, I cannot think of it. In Buddhist practice and in the kitchen, our goal should always be to meet adverse and unpleasant circumstances skillfully, transforming them into something workable and useful. Much of monastery life is spent caring for and treating vegetables for this very reason.

Usually we think of monasteries as sullen, isolated places, filled with monks intent on renouncing the world. This is partially true, as renunciation is a foundational value of monasticism. But monasteries are an integral part of the fabric of society in Asia; they are surrounded by people, seasons, governments, farms, and festivals. Monks tend to the physical and spiritual well-being of their parishioners and are responsible for ushering dead spirits safely into the afterlife. In return, devout laypeople donate food, time, or money — a portion of their yearly rice crop, their best homemade pickles, or leftovers from their shops.

Food donations in particular match the vicissitudes of the seasons. In Japan, since people donated what they grew themselves, we would receive a large number of cabbages and radishes in the winter, plums and bamboo sprouts in the spring, tomatoes and cucumbers in the summer, and mushrooms in the fall. Although of course we appreciated these donations, sometimes we would have only one kind of vegetable to eat. For example, there would be more cucumbers than we could possibly eat, but only cucumbers.

A *togan* is a Japanese melon with a hard texture that is considered a delicacy and usually only found in specialty restaurants. However, some winters we would receive dozens and dozens of *togan*. I remember the basement being filled with small mountains of them. We would eat them breakfast, lunch, and dinner, served all kinds of ways: cooked and then simmered in soy broth, covered with a thickened Chinese sauce, or sliced thin in salads. There was no throwing these vegetables out or giving them away.

Working for years in Japanese kitchens as I did, I came to learn that many Japanese vegetables, especially those considered delicacies, are poisonous or inedible in their natural state. *Umeboshi*, or pickled plums, are made from small plums that are inedible until pickled in salt. I have spent countless hours over a sink peeling off the celery-like skin of *fuki*, or butterbur, which stains your fingers brown. Mountain yams need to be peeled before grating, but the white inside is a skin irritant, so there is a special way to grate the yam without allowing the white part to touch your hands.

Of all the poisonous, inedible, hand-staining, and hand-irritating vegetables I have cooked with, there is a special place in my heart for *takenoko*, or bamboo. In Japan, bamboo shoots are literally weeds; they appear overnight in April and May like crop circles (and sometimes in circles!), and if they are left to proliferate, they will take over entire mountains. They grow at an alarming rate, often doubling in height overnight. Thus, for a few weeks in the spring, people in the countryside spend their days chopping down baby bamboo and then serving up Bamboo Rice (p. 67) or Clear Soup with Bamboo Shoots and Wakame (p. 72).

Despite its delicate, almost nonexistent flavor, bamboo is a dangerous vegetable. Untreated, bamboo is inedible, and even if it is prepared correctly, eating too much bamboo can make people break out in hives. There is a certain ridiculousness to bamboo as well. It has brown, hairy bark that makes it look like an elephant's trunk before you take the bark off in sheets. I've seen bamboo shoots as small as an asparagus stalk and as large as a small dog.

Bamboo can be transformed from an inedible tree into a delicacy worthy of inclusion in soup, stir-fries, stews, or rice by cooking the bamboo trunk in leftover rice water (or water with rice bran added) over low heat for a couple of hours. Using rice water will remove toxins and make the bamboo less bitter. When the bamboo is cool, the brown bark can be peeled off (using rubber gloves, as the bark can irritate hands) to reveal the white center.

Different parts of the bamboo trunk are used for different dishes. The very bottom of the bamboo, ringed by a layer of eerie black bumps, is hard and almost inedible; it is basically a tree. After the black bumps are cut off, the hard flesh underneath can be ground in a food processor, mixed with cornstarch, and made into dumplings. The middle section, also hard, is sliced thin, so that it can be cooked thoroughly in a stir-fry, such as Chinese-style chop-suey, or fried with hot pepper, soy sauce, and sugar. The pointy top part of the bamboo is the softest and most delicious part. If it is very young, it can be eaten without further cooking, with just wasabi and soy sauce. More commonly, though, this soft bamboo shows up in soups or is lightly simmered in soy broth and then arranged with other vegetables such as carrots, shiitake mushrooms, and green beans.

Bamboo is a challenging vegetable. Most Japanese people these days (and Americans who wish to cook with it) buy it preboiled and peeled at the supermarket. But I think this takes the magic out of the whole spring bamboo explosion. There is a certain fun in the immensity of treating bamboo and cooking it yourself — being up to your elbows in hairy bamboo bark and rice bran–colored water. And what is better for Zen practice than converting a giant elephant tusk–like, semipoisonous weed into food?

Many experiences in life seem like unpeeled bamboo — inedible, ridiculous, ugly, and hard. Maybe we hate our job, are struggling in school, or find that our best friend is starting to get on our nerves. And maybe, like an unskilled farmer, we

think the easiest thing is to throw these experiences away —
quit our job, change majors, change friends. But a good cook
knows how to turn even the most terrifying, skin-irritating.
vegetable into a delicacy.

The more experience we have transforming poison into a
meal, the more comfortable we become with difficult conver-
sations, with immense tasks, with facing the unknown. As in
dealing with bamboo, we learn that transforming emotional
poison takes bravery, patience, and, in the beginning, guidance. But once we are used to it, it becomes natural. We come
to respect and understand our life's strange vegetables — the
difficult friends, the unsatisfying careers. We learn to attend
to them with attention and energy. We know what ingredients
to mix in. It is a step-by-step process. It takes time, but it is
not in and of itself difficult. First put the bamboo into a pot.
Then add rice bran and water. The difficulty is in renewing
our intention, in not giving up. In this way, we can transform
any poison into a meal.

If you have finished detoxifying your bamboo — or if you
have bought it preboiled and peeled from a store — the first
dish you will want to make will be Bamboo Rice.

⦿ BAMBOO RICE

Nothing says spring like a bowl of hot Bamboo Rice served
with soup.

Serves 4

> 3 cups uncooked white rice
> 7 ounces boiled and cleaned bamboo (preferably
>   the top part)
> 1 to 2 pieces (2 × 2 inches) *abura age* (fried tofu)

3½ cups dashi
4 tablespoons soy sauce
2 tablespoons sake
1 tablespoon mirin
Pinch of salt

Wash the rice well, and cut the bamboo into thin half-moons. Carefully cut the *abura age* down the middle and open it up like a book so that it doubles in size; then slice it into thin ½-inch-wide strips. Mix together the dashi, soy sauce, sake, mirin, and salt in a saucepan and bring to a boil. Add the bamboo and *abura age* and simmer for 10 minutes. Let the mixture cool down completely, so the bamboo absorbs the flavor.

Put the washed rice into the rice cooker. Remove the tofu and bamboo from the dashi mixture with a slotted spoon and place it on top of the rice in the rice cooker. Add enough of the leftover dashi mixture to the rice cooker, so that the liquid is slightly above the 3-cup line (you will need slightly more than 3 cups of liquid because you are going to cook rice as well as bamboo). Cook the rice for the allotted time.

There is a certain spiritual (and olfactory) satisfaction in transforming a poisonous weed into a meal. And yet no matter how skillful we are as cooks, the body knows bamboo is not to be eaten every day. It is still, fundamentally, a dangerous plant. One year at the monastery when we had an influx of bamboo, the kitchen served it several times a day. Eventually, people started getting sick.

Just as we can pay attention to having just enough money, food, or material objects, it is useful to become aware of when there is too much toxicity in our lives. A little bit of bamboo is wonderful once in a while, but eating it every day can make our skin break out in hives or cause indigestion. Similarly, it's useful to know when the pain of a relationship or the strain of a physical sensation is too much. Sitting in meditation is good, but it's possible to sit for too long and injure ourselves physically. We need to be tuned in to how our body relates to pain and difficulty.

Personally, I have discovered that when I sit for a long time in one position, my body feels cramped and achy. In meditation, if those feelings are due to restlessness, it's useful to sit through them. But there is a different kind of pain, the pain of injuring the body, that also appears when we sit for long periods of time. It is crucial to understand the difference. Sitting through boredom is useful; enduring injury is not.

Some difficult relationships and experiences can be treated like bamboo. We can boil them and transform the poison into a delicacy. This is powerful emotional alchemy. But other relationships will always be toxic. They will grow worse over time, and we only hurt ourselves and others by trying to fix them. It's important to leave this kind of poison behind. The more we pay attention to our bodies and listen deeply, the more we can understand which pain or poison is detrimental and which kind can be useful.

⬤ EIGHT TREASURES STIR-FRY (*HAPPOSAI*)

Chop-suey is technically a Chinese dish, but it frequently appears on Japanese menus, where it is called *happosai*, meaning "eight treasures," for the variety of tasty ingredients, especially the shrimp and pork. Buddhist monks have figured out a way to prepare it without meat or processed soup stock by using shiitake stock, ginger, and sesame oil (the trifecta of Japanese-style vegetarian Chinese flavor), which gives the dish an earthy, rich flavor. Oh, and sugar, but the sugar can be our little secret.

This dish is great served piping hot on a cold winter day

when there are only cabbage and onions in sight, but it really excels in the late spring, when bamboo is plentiful.

At Nisodo, we would make sure to serve this dish during *sesshin*, or an intensive meditation period. During *sesshin* dozens of guests would stay overnight at the temple, so the number of people we had to cook for swelled. *Happosai* lends itself to preparation for large groups, but also somehow feels fancy and decadent, so it always made its way onto the *sesshin* menu. One of the most senior nuns was an émigré from Taiwan, so that may have been another reason!

Serves 3 to 4

> 6 cups chopped Chinese (napa) cabbage,
>   from about ½ medium cabbage
> 3 large dried shiitake mushrooms, soaked
>   overnight in 2 cups water
> 1 tablespoon vegetable oil
> ¼ yellow onion, sliced
> 2 green onions, diagonally sliced, white and
>   green parts separated
> ½ carrot, cut into half-moons
> 1 small Japanese *piman* (green bell pepper),
>   cut into bite-size pieces
> ⅓ cup boiled bamboo, sliced into 1-inch strips
>   (or use canned bamboo)
> 2 tablespoons minced ginger
> 2 tablespoons sake, *divided*
> 2 tablespoons soy sauce
> 2 tablespoons mirin
> 2 teaspoons sugar
> 1 teaspoon seaweed powder, shiitake dashi powder,
>   or salt to taste (optional)

8 pieces (1 inch each) fried *fu* (wheat gluten) or fried
    koyadofu (freeze-dried tofu; optional; see *Koyadofu*
    "Fried Chicken," p. 146)
⅓ cup ginkgo nuts, boiled and shelled (optional)
1½ tablespoons cornstarch or *katakuriko* (potato
    starch)
⅓ cup water
Drizzle of sesame oil
Cooked rice or fried noodles, for serving

Break the cabbage leaves apart. Separate the white and green parts of the leaves: cut the white parts diagonally into bite-size pieces (this makes the white parts easier to chew), and tear or cut the green sections into inch-long pieces. Remove the shiitakes from the soaking liquid and slice thinly. Reserve the shiitake soaking liquid.

Heat the oil in a large skillet on high and stir-fry the sliced yellow onion and white parts of the green onions for 2 minutes, until they have softened slightly. Add the white parts of the cabbage, the carrots, bell pepper, bamboo, and ginger; stir-fry for another minute and then add 1 tablespoon of sake. Sauté the vegetables, stirring frequently, until the sake has completely cooked off, about 2 minutes.

Add the shiitake soaking liquid to the frying pan as well as the soy sauce, mirin, sugar, and remaining tablespoon of sake. Bring to a boil and simmer the vegetables until tender, about 5 minutes. If the cooking stock tastes weak, add a teaspoon of seaweed powder, shiitake dashi powder, and/or salt to taste. When the vegetables are completely tender, add the green cabbage leaves, fried *fu* or *koyadofu*, and ginkgo nuts, if using. Cook for 1 minute.

Dissolve the cornstarch in the ⅓ cup water and stir to combine. When the vegetable mixture is vigorously boiling, add the cornstarch slurry and stir gently until the sauce thickens. Remove the pan from the heat and drizzle with a little bit of sesame oil. Garnish with sliced green onion tops and serve over rice or fried noodles.

Meal Idea: Serve with Crushed Cucumber and Tomato Salad (p. 26) and Clear Soup (below) with cubed silken tofu, wakame, and green onions.

CLEAR SOUP (*SUMASHI*) WITH BAMBOO SHOOTS AND WAKAME

Japanese clear soup, or *sumashi*, is one of the great joys in life. It draws its power from a healthy amount of salt and is meant to serve as a kind of palate cleanser to offset more complex dishes. I remember learning to cook *sumashi* at Nisodo. Unsure if I had made it right, I asked an older nun for help. She tasted the soup and then added a generous shake of salt. Unsatisfied, she added even more salt and then tasted again.

"Delicious," she concluded. "There shouldn't be too much soy sauce," she added. "Otherwise it will no longer be clear. The flavor comes from sake, *konbu*, and salt."

Sumashi is a soup for celebrating and serving to guests, because it is a highly visual soup that is almost more for presentation than for taste. In Japan, it is usually served in red lacquered bowls with lids. The broth is completely clear — unlike with noodle soup or stew, how the soup looks is paramount. In this version, it's best to use the freshest, smallest, most tender bamboo shoots you can find. Remember to buy the bamboo preboiled or boil it yourself before adding it to this soup. Fresh wakame (edible seaweed) works best in *sumashi*, but since that is very difficult to obtain, dried wakame can also be used.

Don't expect fireworks from *sumashi*. It's more like a bright, cloudless sky.

Serves 3

> 3 cups *konbu* dashi, or 1½ teaspoons *konbu* dashi
>   powder dissolved in 3 cups water
> 1½ teaspoons soy sauce
> ½ cup sake
> 1 tablespoon mirin
> ½ to 1 teaspoon salt
> 9 thinly sliced pieces bamboo (half-moons or rounds)
>   from the top inch of the stalk
> 1 tablespoon dried wakame (seaweed)
> A few sprigs of *mitsuba*, *sansho*, or other fragrant herbs,
>   for garnish

Bring the dashi to a boil in a medium saucepan. Add soy sauce, sake, and mirin and reduce to a simmer. Stir and allow the flavors to combine for a minute while the stock simmers. Taste, and then add salt if desired, starting with ½ teaspoon and working up to 1 whole teaspoon (this will depend on whether you are using dashi powder; you will need to add less salt with dashi powder, since the sodium content is already high).

Add the bamboo and wakame and simmer gently for 1 to 2 minutes, until the wakame is completely reconstituted and soft. Pour into bowls, distributing the bamboo evenly between the bowls, and serve piping hot. Garnish with *mitsuba* or *sansho*, if using.

Variations: A variety of combinations of other vegetables can be substituted for the bamboo in this soup. Unlike miso soup, which is quite chunky, *sumashi* should be delicate and works best if the ingredients are sliced very thin. Some vegetable ideas for Clear Soup include:

- Green beans sliced thinly on the diagonal, sliced *abura age* (fried tofu), and wakame (seaweed)

- Enoki (or shimeji) mushrooms and sliced green onions
- Enoki mushrooms and wakame
- Shimeji (or any) mushrooms and colorful *fu* (wheat gluten), garnished with *mitsuba*
- Cubed silken tofu, wakame, and green onions
- Cubed silken tofu, wakame, and sliced snap peas
- Cubed silken tofu, garnished with *mitsuba*
- Thinly sliced daikon (in quarter-moons) and shimeji mushrooms, garnished with yuzu (Japanese lemon) peel
- Thinly sliced daikon (in quarter-moons), spinach, and shimeji mushrooms
- Thinly sliced daikon and carrot (in quarter-moons) and deep-fried mochi (rice cake)
- Julienned daikon and julienned carrot, garnished with *mitsuba*
- Spinach, cubed silken tofu, and shimeji mushrooms
- Thinly sliced okra, cubed silken tofu, enoki mushrooms, and green onions
- Colorful *fu* in a flower shape, garnished with *mitsuba*
- Any small Asian dumplings cooked in broth

5

BALANCE

How to Find Harmony
of Flavor and Priorities

I practiced at Nisodo for three years until I realized that my life was out of balance. At that point, I had been in the monastic system for a total of five years. I was working as hard as I could, dedicating my life to Buddhism and the spiritual community, but I could tell there were parts of myself that were underdeveloped. I was still quick to anger, still lonely. I wanted to study and write, to form intimate relationships, and to travel, and I could tell that the way I was living did not make these things possible.

In his book *A Path with Heart*, Buddhist teacher and psychotherapist Jack Kornfield writes about "spiritual bypassing," the dangerous trap of using spirituality to avoid our difficult or shameful emotions. He warns: "We may have been taught that experiences we have at the 'spiritual' level in meditation, as if by magic, will have the power to transform all the other levels of our being. Thus, if we have a great 'awakening'...we think this will be enough to change our vision, heal our hearts, and bring us into harmony."

Of course, this isn't true. This observation, that spiritual practitioners often believe meditation or awakening will magically transform their lives, is something that took me many years of intensive Buddhist practice to understand. I often expected Buddhist teachers to be fully perfect, realized beings and was shocked and disappointed when I discovered that in their personal lives they were often inattentive, forgetful, fearful of emotional vulnerability, impatient, or even cruel. It was not until I left the monastery, started going to therapy, and began reforming relationships that I realized my spiritual practice had not touched large aspects of my being.

Kornfield's language of "compartments" is particularly useful. He uses the concept of compartmentalization to explain how meditation or spiritual practice touches some parts of ourselves while sequestering others. For example, he notes, "Because awareness does not automatically transfer itself from one dimension of our life to another, compartments remain in the areas where our fears, our wounds, and our defenses are deepest." In myself, I noticed that although Zen practice helped me to strengthen wisdom, endurance, and clarity, it did not help me address either my own insecurities related to money and work or the underlying issues of shame and self-hatred. It is only now, at the age of thirty-two, that I am beginning to construct a professional identity for myself and really tackle the problem of inner shame.

Although becoming a Buddhist nun was a profound, life-changing experience that was probably necessary for me at age twenty-four, it was also a way I could avoid dealing with the gnarly questions of how to show up in society, how to earn money, how to be in an intimate relationship, and what social identity I wanted to inhabit. In other words, as a Buddhist nun I could compartmentalize my insecurities about money and work by taking a vow of poverty. I could compartmentalize the fear and frustration I felt in romantic relationships with men by being celibate. I could also compartmentalize my self-esteem issues by relying on the Buddhist notion that there is no self. I could focus on helping others and "detaching from my ego" as a way to avoid addressing my self-hatred.

I believe spiritual practice is ultimately about balance, about finding a middle way. It is said that spirituality focuses on the light, while psychotherapy focuses on shadow. It is clear to me that we need both, that we need a balance of light and dark, just as we need a balance of flavors and a balance between discipline and abandon. We need to be able to mediate between our small, conditioned self and the larger, transcendent one. Both selves, both ways of being, are  important. Some people live their whole lives trapped inside a very narrow, conditioned view of who they are. That is a shame. And others try to bypass themselves and their shadows to become saints. I know, because I have been both of those people.

Balance is often a moving target, but we know when our lives are out of balance. We know when we have been sitting inside for too long or when too much of our emotion is invested in a particular project. It can be helpful to be intentional about where we are putting our time and energy, to purposefully carve out time for the things that give us joy as well as the work that needs to be done. I am happiest when I can follow some kind of schedule. Schedules, like flavor rules, are meant to be broken. But it's good to know the rules before you break them.

Years later, I am just as proud of myself for leaving monastery life as I am for entering it. I believe we know what we need to grow and flourish and that these things change throughout our life. It is as if we have a scale inside our heart that measures feelings, thoughts, and experiences. At first, the scale is difficult to read because we don't even believe it is there. But if we trust that our hearts are worth listening to — that we deserve to make choices — it can guide us to a way of being that navigates extremes.

Once you have prepared fluffy, shiny rice and understand how to make subtle yet savory dashi, you can build your Japanese meal on this foundation. A good Japanese meal — like a good meal anywhere — should be well balanced. It should not have too much oil and should have dishes that contain all the five tastes: sweet, salty, sour, bitter, and umami. Here are some examples of the five tastes:

- **Sweet:** carrot, pumpkin, fruit, and sweeteners such as sugar and mirin
- **Salty:** miso, soy sauce, salt
- **Sour:** vinegar, *umeboshi* (pickled plums)
- **Bitter:** mountain vegetables (ostrich fern, butterbur stalks, etc.); *nabana* (Japanese rapeseed blossom); bitter gourds such as *goya*; some versions of the five tastes list spicy as a taste instead of bitter, so we might include mustard, wasabi, and chili in this category as well
- **Umami:** seaweed, mushrooms, fish, cheese

The best cooks I encountered in Japan also strove to balance the "five colors" in the presentation of the dish. The five colors are white, yellow, green, red (or orange), and brown/black (or purple).

Traditionally, a Japanese meal is rice, soup, pickles, and any number of side dishes, so with a little forethought it is actually not so hard to create a meal with all five tastes and all five colors. Start with a base of white rice. This is (obviously) white in color. Next add Miso Soup (p. 54), perhaps with pumpkin, fried tofu, and sliced green onions — this will take care of the salty taste, as miso is quite salty, and the pumpkin provides the sweet taste as well as the yellow color. (You get the idea.) Serve the rice and soup with *takiawase*, or Five-Color Stewed Vegetables.

● FIVE-COLOR STEWED VEGETABLES (*TAKIAWASE*)

Takiawase is a style of Japanese cooking in which vegetables are cooked separately, allowing each vegetable to retain the purity of its flavor, and then served together in the same dish. When you have special guests over (or, if you are a monk, when you have people come to the temple to learn zazen on the weekend), serve this luxurious and beautifully arranged *takiawase* of stuffed *abura age*, daikon, carrot, shiitakes, and snap peas. This contains the colors of orange (carrots), dark brown/black (mushrooms), white (daikon), yellow (*abura age*), and green (snap peas). The stewed shiitake mushrooms also add an extra burst of umami.

I find the taste of whole shiitakes a little overpowering, so I like to stew them in a very sweet broth. Simmering the carrot slowly in sweet broth also helps it retain its beautiful orange color. However, if you are wary of sugar and not afraid of the mushroom taste, you can stew everything in the kind of soy-based broth used for the daikon. In Japan, this dish usually calls for snap peas, but green beans can also be used.

Serves 4

> 1 piece (4 inches long) daikon, cut into 1-inch pieces
> Leftover water from washing rice (or fresh water with ¼ cup rice added)
> ½ carrot, cut into 1-inch pieces
> 4 small dried shiitake mushrooms or 2 larger ones cut in half, soaked overnight in enough water to cover
> 3 snap peas (or green beans)
> 4 pieces (2 × 2 inches each) *abura age* (fried tofu)
> 1 mochi (rice cake), cut into small cubes
> 2 tablespoons diced cooked carrot
> 1 dried shiitake mushroom, soaked overnight in water and finely minced

Broth for the Daikon
> 3 cups dashi
> 3 tablespoons soy sauce
> 1 tablespoon sake
> 2 tablespoons mirin
> 1 teaspoon sugar
> ¼ teaspoon salt

Broth for the Carrot
> 1 cup dashi
> 2 tablespoons sugar
> 1 teaspoon salt

Broth for the Shiitakes
> ½ cup dashi
> 1 tablespoon sugar
> 1 tablespoon soy sauce

Broth for the *Abura Age* Pouches
  2 cups dashi
  2 tablespoons soy sauce
  2 teaspoons sugar

Cut off about ¼ inch of the outer skin of the daikon pieces. With a knife, make two slits to form an *X* in the center of each piece. Bring the leftover rice water to a boil in a medium saucepan, add the daikon pieces, and cook for about 20 minutes to remove bitterness. Rinse off the cloudy rice water and place the daikon in another pot. Add the dashi, soy sauce, sake, mirin, sugar, and salt. Simmer gently for 10 minutes and then remove the pot from the heat. As the daikon cools, it will absorb the flavor of the broth.

Meanwhile, in a small saucepan on the lowest possible heat, slowly simmer the carrot pieces in the dashi, sugar, and salt for 10 to 20 minutes, until tender, and then remove the pan from the heat.

Remove the whole shiitakes from the soaking liquid. In a saucepan bring the dashi, sugar, and soy sauce to a boil and add the shiitakes. Cook on medium for 5 minutes or until tender (watch it carefully, as the broth may suddenly caramelize, leaving the mushrooms to burn!).

Blanch the snap peas whole in salted water for 1 to 2 minutes, until just tender. Drain and place immediately in a bowl of ice water. Once cooled, remove the peas from the water and slice in half on the diagonal.

To make the stuffed *abura age*, cut off the top half inch of each *abura age* piece lengthwise (you can save the part you cut off for soup). Start opening the *abura age* by taking a small sharp knife and making a slit in the top, where the white part of the tofu is exposed. Then, using your fingers, carefully open up the *abura age*, so that it resembles a small pouch. Stuff each pouch with the cubed mochi, diced cooked carrot, and minced shiitake. To close the pouch, weave a toothpick in and out across the opening. In a small saucepan bring the dashi, soy sauce, and sugar to a boil. Stand the four pouches next to each other in the pot, leaning them against each other so they don't fall down. Cook for 5 minutes.

Remove the vegetables and *abura age* pouches from their broth and distribute them equally between four dishes. Add the snap peas. Ladle a spoonful of the daikon's broth into each dish.

Variation: You can substitute cubed kabocha (Japanese pumpkin) and sliced bamboo shoots for the daikon, cooking them separately in the dashi and flavorings used for the daikon above.

Meal Ideas: Serve with a vinegar dish, such as Cucumber and Bean Sprout Salad (below) or Julienned Daikon and Carrot in Sweet Vinegar Sauce (p. 156), and pickles, such as pickled burdock root, for a slight bitter contrast to the sweet, salty, sour, and umami. If you can't find Japanese pickles, a cold salad of blanched broccolini or rapeseed in a mustard, soy, and dashi dressing will provide just enough bitterness.

◉ CUCUMBER AND BEAN SPROUT SALAD

Cucumber and Bean Sprout Salad is best served cold. Since it tastes vinegary, it goes well with salty or spicy dishes.

Serves 4 as a side dish

2 cucumbers, julienned
1½ teaspoons salt
5 cups *moyashi* (bean sprouts)
4 green onions, sliced diagonally into 1-inch pieces
Sesame seeds, for garnish

Dressing
4 teaspoons sesame oil
3 tablespoons rice vinegar
2 teaspoons soy sauce
2 teaspoons sugar

Salt the cucumbers and let them sit for 10 minutes. Squeeze out excess water from the cucumbers. Make sure to squeeze thoroughly; otherwise the dressing will become diluted with cucumber juice.

To a small pot of salted boiling water, add the bean sprouts and cook for 30 seconds to 1 minute, until just tender. Drain and rinse with cold water. Firmly squeeze out all the water, as with the cucumbers.

In a small bowl mix the sesame oil, vinegar, soy sauce, and sugar well. In a large bowl combine the cucumbers, bean sprouts, and green onions. Add the dressing and mix to combine. Garnish with sesame seeds. This dish will probably not need extra salt, as the cucumbers are already quite salty.

● QUICK JAPANESE CABBAGE PICKLES

Sio zuke, or "salt pickling," is the easiest and quickest way to get Japanese pickles. These quick ginger-flavored pickles can be served as an accompaniment to rice and soup. If you like, add a drizzle of sesame oil at the end to make it more like a salad.

Serves 4 to 6 as a side dish

>1 piece (1 × 1 inch) *konbu* (dried kelp)
>1 small or ½ large Chinese (napa) cabbage
>   (about 8 cups cut into bite-size pieces)
>2 tablespoons finely julienned ginger
>¼ carrot, julienned
>1½ tablespoons salt
>Soy sauce and sesame oil (optional)

Soak the *konbu* in water to cover for 1 hour. Remove it from the water and cut it into thin strips with scissors.

Break the cabbage leaves apart. Separate the white and green parts of the leaves. Cut the cabbage crosswise, the white parts into ½-inch-wide pieces and the leaves into 1-inch-wide pieces.

Place the cabbage in a bowl and then add the *konbu*, ginger, and carrots. Add the salt a little bit at a time, massaging it into the cabbage with your fingers and mixing thoroughly, so that each cabbage leaf has been massaged with salt. Place a plate on top of the cabbage mixture and put a weight on top. Cover everything with a plastic bag and let it sit in the refrigerator at least 5 hours or overnight.

Remove the cabbage mixture from the refrigerator and squeeze out any excess water (there will be a lot pooled at the bottom of the bowl). The pickles are ready to eat, or you can add a bit of soy sauce (depending on how salty the pickles are) and/or a drizzle of sesame oil for a deeper flavor.

6

JUST ENOUGH LUST

How to Add Spice to Your Life (and Dumplings)

To make *gyoza* — Japanese dumplings — you need either meat or a pungent herb like garlic. This is a fact. Oh, of course you could make them with just cabbage and carrots and dip them in plain soy sauce, but why would you want to do that? You would just be eating a mouthful of cabbage. Life is too short to eat plain cabbage dumplings.

In Buddhist monasteries in Japan, garlic is banned because it is said to increase sexual desire, and also because of the smell. But a little of both of these is good once in a while. As a nun, I went for years without eating garlic — and I mean this in more than one way. Monastic living is necessarily simple, and it lacks the kind of spice, fun, and excitement most of us are used to in modern living.

I spent three years training as a nun in Nisodo, the women's monastery. Before that, I lived at another monastery for over a year. I had enthusiastically signed up for what I thought would be a lifetime of nunhood. At age twenty-four, when I was ordained, I wanted a future living in a beautiful temple in the mountains. In this fantasy future, I imagined waking up early to sweep the floor, gazing out over the hazy valley, and eating rice for breakfast. I would have time to write and spend in nature.

Partly I was attracted to that lifestyle because I like quiet. I'm an introvert, and I am naturally comfortable when I am alone. In meditation, I touched a depth of calm and joy that didn't compare with anything I'd known previously. I desperately wanted that kind of peace, so I held on to it the only way I knew how: by committing for life. Throughout the day, there were of course challenges. I couldn't speak Japanese at first, I had trouble following all the rules, and the long hours of physical labor were taxing. But for the first time in my life, I felt as though I knew what I was put on earth to do. I was intoxicated with faith and certainty.

Yet monastery life in Japan is hardly peaceful and quiet. The morning begins with two hours of meditation, but after that come chanting, cleaning, and breakfast, followed by more work. There's always some senior nun bossing you around, so you have to talk to and interact with her a lot, and then maybe you'll gossip about her to the other nuns. There are classes on philosophy and history. There is tea time, which is often an hour long. You eat cakes and cookies, fight over the best jobs in the temple, talk about the families you've left behind, and exchange gifts of incense, prayer beads, socks, and girly notepads and pens.

A funny thing about the spiritual life is that it is fairly easy to give up physical comforts and pleasure. Food, sex, alcohol, television, doing my hair, Western clothes — I renounced these willingly and easily. The other monks and nuns around me had as well; or I should say, the nuns did. In Japan, most male monastics marry. During Japan's Meiji Revolution, a period of intense modernization and industrialization in the late 1800s, the government decriminalized marriage and eating meat for Buddhist monks. To this day, Buddhist monks usually marry, while nuns for the most part do not. This is for several reasons — two short ones are that Japanese nuns would rather be single and there is a double standard.

It is fairly easy to give up everything and live your life feeling that you are doing the right thing because you are doing good religious work. And yet the desires and problems that drive us to the spiritual life — those pesky parts of human experience — never really go away. How could they? The human condition does not end. The desires and problems simply change shape. In a modern city, our problems might include job issues, arguments with our spouse, not enough sex, not the right kind of sex, annoying coworkers, and dirty dishes. Inside a monastery the problems are loneliness, jealousy, squabbling with other people, wanting to be the best or most holy, and dirty dishes. Everywhere you go there will be dirty dishes.

I spent years grappling with the various contradictions of Japanese monastery life — which is of course a microcosm of the contradictions in the human experience. I wanted peace and quiet but got gossip and criticism. I wanted wisdom and compassion but got frustration and jealousy. After many years I was able to reconcile these contradictions, in a way. I found that I could find fulfillment even amid the long hours of cleaning, the never-ending rules, the personality clashes. This was because I came to see that Zen practice is about everyday life. It is about doing your best in the situation in front of you, no matter what it is. It is about living a full life based not on external conditions, but the quality of your own character and engagement.

Yet eventually I had a nagging feeling I couldn't shake that I was missing out. For one thing, I was profoundly lonely. Loneliness is almost inevitable for monks and nuns; they've signed up for an isolated monastic existence separate from society. Still, for most clergy the role of family and loved ones is supposed to be re-created by the rest of the monastic community. Humans are social creatures. Even nuns need other human beings around. In Buddhism, the word *sangha* denotes the community of practitioners. The sangha is so important that it is referred to, along with Buddha and dharma, as one of the "three jewels," or cornerstones, of Buddhism. In other words, community is as important as the Buddha and truth itself!

As a foreigner living in Japan, I never felt as though I belonged. Japan is racially monolithic and values "pure" Japaneseness. It is difficult even for Chinese and Korean immigrants to find a place in Japanese society. Being young, white, and American, I felt even more out of place. At the monastery, I was often not allowed to do certain jobs or hold training positions, even though I spoke Japanese, because of my accent. When I was in charge of running the kitchen, people making deliveries or other nuns needing to coordinate something would rarely talk to me; they preferred going through another Japanese person. For a few months a nun in charge of temple funds would not allow non-Japanese nuns to purchase groceries, because she felt that foreigners could not be trusted with money. So even as I felt as though I had found my calling, I was also excluded. I was never allowed to forget that I was an outsider.

There was also a lot of life I wanted to experience. I was twenty-four when I became a nun. My spiritual calling was sincere. But I also wanted to study, work at a real job, write books, have friends, and be in love. After many years of monastic practice, I felt somewhat like the Little Mermaid when she sings about wanting to be where the people are.

There's no good way to rationalize my wish to leave the monastery. I was filled with desire, desire for life, for pleasure, for experience, for cities at night, for fried chicken, and for human contact. During the last weeklong meditation intensive I sat before I left the convent, for about seven hours a day I fantasized about buying red stilettos. We sat in silence from 4:00 AM until bedtime, and I spent a big portion of that time thinking about red shoes.

I let desire push me out of the convent walls and back into the modern world. And when I was out, you better believe I bought some red heels.

After I left the convent, I lived and worked in Japan for another year and a half, studying Japanese and gradually reintegrating myself into contemporary society. I started a blog, wrote articles, memorized kanji (Chinese characters), and had two misadvised flings with two different white libertarian men whose goal in life seemed to be making as much money and dating as many women as possible. It was a confusing time.

My blog became increasingly popular with American Buddhists, and I started to accumulate a fair number of fans. Sometimes I would ask for money on my blog, and readers would comply. But I was still incredibly poor and virtually alone in a foreign country. I knew I didn't want to go back to a Japanese monastery, but I didn't know what else to do. Unsure and unfocused, I applied to master's programs in East Asian studies, with the intent of studying Buddhism academically. I've always liked school and been good at it. I like reading, writing, and thinking. Eventually I was accepted to a fellowship at the University of Southern California and moved back to the United States.

When I moved back to the United States, I planned to

spend six months at the San Francisco Zen Center before I started graduate school. Within the first week I met a man there. He was a fan of my writing and had a kind of celebrity crush on me. He invited me to dinner, and I said yes.

Spoiler alert: I married him.

In a fairy tale I remember from childhood, a king asks his three daughters how much they love him. The youngest daughter says, "I love you like fresh meat loves salt." He is angry and sends her away, but years later he eats at a banquet that uses no salt, and the food is so bland he cannot eat it. At that moment he realizes he has made a mistake, and that his youngest daughter loves him the most.

Human beings need salt. We need a little fire and garlic; we need to rage and dance and cry as much as we need silence and temperance. Loving this man after so many years of silence and loneliness was like tasting garlic and salt after a lifetime of tasteless food. It was so delicious I knew I would rather have the whole meal and all its consequences than go back to being noble, safe, and correct.

It has been two years, and I am still waiting for the other shoe to drop. I am still waiting for the pain and suffering I have been told follows greed. The Buddha preached that for those with an impure mind, suffering follows greed "like a wheel follows the ox that draws the cart." My husband and I are not perfect. He gets jealous and gives too much. I am greedy for affection and get angry easily. But I also know that my desire, anger, and love are colors in a larger tapestry, part of the richness of living a full life. I know that this fullness brings me closer to the truth, not farther away from it, and it is a unique, quiet truth, not a big, universal one for the philosophy books. It is simply my truth.

I no longer believe romantic love contradicts Buddhist practice. I have lived inside the tornado of contradiction for so long that it has subsided to paradox. Whereas contradiction is painful and unsettling, paradox is light and full of wonder, almost humorous. Paradox and contradiction are often so close together we cannot see the difference. But if we recognize contradiction for what it is, if we allow contradiction to remain unresolved long enough within our heart, it can change shape. It opens like a tornado dissolving into the sky.

There are some benefits to misbehaving.

Obon is a yearly festival in Japan when people gather to honor their dead family members. Most Japanese families have an altar with memorial tablets dedicated to ancestors, and during *obon* they place on it fruit, rice, candy, or any kind of food their family members enjoyed while they were alive. Because it is said that ancestors visit their family's houses during *obon*, traditionally Japanese also decorate these altars with cucumbers and eggplants made to resemble horses and cows, so that the ancestors can ride back and forth between this realm and the next. The vegetable animals usually have "legs" made out of toothpicks.

The abbess of Nisodo once told a story about being in a family's home and noticing a particularly crooked eggplant on the altar. Because of its extreme bend, it looked like an especially realistic cow. "Sometimes it's good to be crooked," the abbess said. The father of the family quipped, "Maybe there's hope for me after all!"

Crooked eggplants are good sometimes, and sometimes pungency is good in food. Everything in life need not be straight and simple. At my new home in Los Angeles, years after leaving the convent, I tried making vegetarian *gyoza* without garlic. I really did. And they were fine. Perfectly fine, but missing something important, missing that little taste that makes the difference between "fine" and wanting to eat more of it.

Eventually I remembered the missing ingredient. In Japan, I learned to make *gyoza* with cabbage, ginger, and *nira*. *Nira* are Japanese garlic chives; they look like green onions, with long green strap-shaped leaves, but they are far more pungent than green onions. Chopped into small pieces and mashed into cabbage by hand, they make the whole mass of vegetables sticky. They are what make *gyoza* taste like *gyoza* — they are like the bend in an eggplant, the red stilettos for a twenty-seven-year-old nun.

◉ DUMPLINGS (*GYOZA*)

You can find *nira* if you look hard enough. A Japanese grocery will probably sell them. A Korean market might also have them. If you can't find *nira*, then you will just have to use garlic, won't you? But if you can find *nira*, and I hope you do, you could make these *gyoza*.

Makes 20 dumplings

> 1½ cups shredded Chinese (napa) cabbage
>   (or cut into thin bite-size strips)
> ¾ cup finely chopped *nira* (garlic chives)
> 1 piece (1 inch) ginger, finely chopped
> 1 teaspoon sesame oil
> 1 teaspoon soy sauce
> Salt
> 20 *gyoza* (dumpling) wrappers

Place the cabbage in a large bowl. Add the *nira* and mix. Using your hands, mash the *nira* and cabbage together for several minutes until it becomes sticky. Add the ginger, sesame oil, soy sauce, and a healthy shake of salt. Stir to combine.

To make *gyoza*, place one wrapper on your left palm. Spoon about 1 tablespoon of the filling onto the wrapper. Wet the index finger of your right hand and use it to wet the outside rim of the *gyoza* wrapper. Fold the wrapper over until the wet edges are touching and press the edges together (this may take some practice; you will want to balance the *gyoza* and press only the edges, so that the filling doesn't squirt out). Crimp the edges of the wrapper, starting at the middle and working your way to the right edge and then working from the middle to the left edge. Reshape the whole dumpling so that it looks like a half-moon with a flat bottom.

The easiest way to cook *gyoza* is to boil them. They are delicious pan-fried, but you should probably not attempt this unless your dumplings are impeccably made and you are confident in your frying skills. Boil the *gyoza* in plain water for 1 to 2 minutes, until the wrappers are translucent. Or better yet, make a Chinese-style broth with dashi, finely chopped ginger, garlic, soy sauce, sake, and a drizzle of sesame or chili oil. Add Chinese cabbage, onions, and any other vegetables you like.

Once the soup is prepared, add the *gyoza* at the last minute and boil for 1 to 2 minutes or until cooked through.

● PERFECT BOK CHOI

How about some perfect bok choi? Much like Rapunzel's birth mother, I often crave bitter greens, and Perfect Bok Choi is what I make when I want a huge helping of vegetables over rice. These bok choi are so good that my husband will eat them without complaining, which is saying a lot for a bok choi recipe. My method here combines a healthy appreciation for garlic with the spirit of the *nimono* cooking technique (boiling first and then adding flavor later to retain the shape of the vegetable). I wanted to eat bok choi the way they are served in Chinese restaurants and started making them this way upon returning to the United States.

Serves 2 to 3

> 6 baby bok choi
> 1½ teaspoons vegetable oil
> 2 cloves garlic, minced
> 1½ teaspoons sugar
> 1 tablespoon soy sauce
> 3 tablespoons water
> ⅛ teaspoon dashi powder
> Salt to taste

Cut off the bottom ½ inch of the bok choi, but keep the rest intact. Blanch the bok choi in salted water for 1 to 2 minutes, until the white part of the vegetable can be pierced easily with a fork but is still crisp. Drain.

Meanwhile, in a separate pan on medium, heat the oil and sauté the garlic until it begins to emit an aroma, stirring frequently, about 2 minutes. In a small bowl combine the sugar, soy sauce, water, and dashi powder and then add this mixture to the pan of garlic. Cook on high for another 2 minutes, stirring frequently, until the sauce thickens slightly.

Arrange the cooked bok choi on a plate and drizzle the garlic sauce on top. Add salt to taste.

Meal Idea: Serve on top of a big bowl of rice.

MARINATED FRIED EGGPLANT (*NASU AGEDASHI*)

Japanese eggplants are plentiful in the summer. Marinated Fried Eggplant is a luxurious, savory dish that is appropriate for when you need to impress your guests. Deep-fried eggplant is cooled in a sweet soy-flavored broth and garnished with grated ginger and daikon radish. Served on a green *shiso* leaf, with an intricate crisscross pattern on the eggplant skin, this side dish looks especially beautiful.

Like Fried Tofu in Sauce (p. 57), we would often make *nasu agedashi* when guests came to the temple. I have so many memories of slicing crisscrosses into heaps and heaps of eggplant, and I'll always remember how they looked, deep-fried and coated in sauce, against the green *shiso* leaf on a blue-and-white ceramic dish.

Serves 4 as a side dish (two pieces per person)

2 long purple *nasu* (Japanese eggplants)
3 cups dashi
2 teaspoons mirin
1 teaspoon sugar
3 tablespoons soy sauce
Vegetable oil for deep-frying
Dash of salt

4 *shiso* leaves (optional)
¼ cup grated daikon
2 teaspoons grated ginger

Cut the tops off the eggplants. Cut each eggplant in half first lengthwise, then widthwise, creating four pieces per eggplant. Using a sharp knife, make a series of diagonal slits in the skin of the eggplant pieces, piercing at least ¼ inch deep (you should be able to fit 10 to 12 slits on the skin of each piece). Repeat the process going the opposite direction, creating a lattice pattern on the skin of each eggplant piece. This will help the eggplant cook all the way through and absorb flavor.

Mix together the dashi, mirin, sugar, and soy sauce in a large saucepan. Bring to a boil and remove the pan from the heat.

Pour at least 1½ inches of oil into a large deep pan and heat to between 350 and 370°F. (Or if you have a deep-fryer, use it following the manufacturer's directions.) When hot, add the eggplant, skin side down. Fry for about 4 minutes, until the skin begins to darken ever so slightly, and then flip and fry on the other side until golden brown.

Reheat the broth to boiling (this should only take a few seconds) and add a dash of salt. Place the cooked eggplant on a plate covered with paper towels briefly to absorb excess oil and then place the eggplant in the broth. Remove the saucepan from the heat. This dish can be served either hot or cold, but if you allow the eggplant to cool completely in the broth, it will become especially flavorful.

To serve, place a *shiso* leaf on each of four small plates. Place two eggplant pieces on top of each *shiso* leaf and then spoon a bit of grated daikon and grated ginger onto the eggplant. For more flavor, drizzle another spoonful of the broth over the eggplant.

Meal Idea: Serve with rice; Miso Soup (p. 54) with potatoes, yellow onions, and carrots; and Cold Vegetables with Tofu Dressing (p. 43).

7

CALIFORNIA

How to Cook and Live
Where You Are

In Japan there is a proverb, *Go ni heite wa go ni shittegai*. This translates literally as, "When entering the country, obey the laws of the country," but it has the same general meaning as "When in Rome, do as the Romans do." In the West, we usually say "When in Rome" when we are on vacation or trying out something new and challenging we wouldn't normally do. In Japan, though, people use it to describe the importance of obeying local manners and customs.

When I first moved to Japan, the monks and nuns would often scold me with this proverb as a way to convince me to conform to Japanese customs ("Why do we have to eat dishes in separate bowls?" "*Go ni heite wa go ni shittegai!*"). I never expected that I would have to put this proverb into practice in the United States, my own country, but as it turned out, readjusting to life in America was more challenging than I expected. Returning Peace Corps volunteers are well aware of a phenomenon called "reverse culture shock," in which one's own culture feels foreign and disorienting. Although I didn't feel reverse culture shock per se, I found that returning to the United States required me to let go of my ideas and opinions all over again.

In the spring of 2016, I moved back to the United States. A few months before flying back to San Francisco, I had contacted the guest manager at City Center, the downtown location of the San Francisco Zen Center (SFZC), to see about practicing there as a guest student. I had approximately $500 to my name and thought it would be good to practice in an American Zen center after all that time in Japan. The guest manager told me I was welcome to apply to be a guest student and stay for a few weeks.

A week before leaving Japan, I wrote again to confirm my stay. To my surprise, the guest-manager position at City Center was held by a new person, who informed me that although I could stay for ten days, there were no beds available after that. In a panic, I wrote to the guest manager at Green Gulch Farm, another of the SFZC's locations, in Marin County, near San Francisco, whom I knew from a brief stay a few years earlier. After some pleading emails, she managed to secure me a spot as a kitchen apprentice that would begin after my ten-day stay at City Center.

At City Center I shared a room with two other female students, a former kayaking instructor in her twenties who was having a very relatable existential crisis and a somewhat off-kilter middle-aged woman whom I could never figure out (and who probably was having a midlife crisis; Buddhist centers seem to attract people in crisis). The room smelled of mildew and the sheets were worn thin, but I was happy to have a real bed for the first time in years (as opposed to a futon).

The other two women and I were put to work performing housekeeping and other odd tasks around the building. City Center calls itself a temple and has the official designation of "temple" with the Japanese Soto Zen bureaucracy, but it feels more like a boarding school — a massive compound with a series of dormitories and communal bathrooms attached to a zendo (meditation hall), kitchen, and chanting hall. In the mornings we would wake early to sit zazen and chant, as in Japan, and after breakfast we would mop the hallways, clean the zendo, or sweep the dining room. There was an hour-long break after lunch whose duration felt positively luxurious.

I knew when I signed up to stay at City Center that the life-style would be different from the one in Japan. Even though the practice is the same, Americans do it a bit differently — there's more emphasis on personal emotion and fulfillment in the West, less emphasis on ceremony and manners. I was in an odd state of mind those first few weeks. I had received Dharma transmission only a week or two before — a week-long complicated and secret ceremony certifying me to teach Zen and signifying the end of monastic training, at least on paper.

I didn't tell anyone about this, because I was trying to be humble, have a beginner's mind, and throw myself into work. Yet I couldn't help but feel the contrast between what I had trained to be and how I was presenting myself; it felt like act-ing. Additionally, as someone outside of the "San Francisco Zen Center lineage," I felt out of place and awkward. Most of the priests training there are ordained by other SFZC teachers, and there is no clear trajectory for outsiders, like me, who are (unofficially) disallowed from holding positions of authority.

But the weeks I spent at City Center were also a time of ex-citement and joy. I quickly fell for a man living there, Gensan.

I had brought him a calligraphy from Japan to say thank you for donating to my blog, and he asked me to dinner.

"What do I wear?" I asked him.

"You can borrow a shirt of mine if you don't have any other clothes," he offered. I was still shaving my head and wearing mostly black monastic clothing.

"I have *shirts*," I retorted, although most of the shirts I had were from the center's donation box. I had thrown away most of my clothes when I was ordained, but I still had a black dress that I had worn to a friend's funeral almost a decade earlier. I paired that with black ballet flats and a used denim jacket that I had bought from a thrift store earlier that week. My head was shaved almost down to the skin, but I looked pretty, in a kind of vulnerable and mentally unhinged way.

I was unsure if our plans constituted a date, but simultaneously I also knew that I was a woman and he was a man and he had asked me to dinner. Walking to meet him, I was filled with nervous excitement. We met near Golden Gate Park and walked through the trees up to Stow Lake and through the park. We chatted so easily, it was as if we had known each other for years; at first we talked about Buddhism, but soon he was telling me about his recent divorce and I was lamenting the confusion of my sort-of love life.

We fell for each other fast. We stayed up late texting each other and stole away any chance we had to go on long walks. We would sit on park benches, and afterward he would buy me ice cream. A few weeks later he gave me a book with an inscription that was signed "Love."

"It just felt right!" he protested, embarrassed.

At the end of ten days, my visiting student status expired and I had to move out of City Center and into Green Gulch Farm, a Zen center and organic farm in Marin County. At Green Gulch I began the kitchen apprenticeship program, a several-month training program for beginning students wishing to learn about Zen and get hands-on experience with food prep and vegetarian cooking.

I was happy to be back in the kitchen. Cooking has always been the way I connect best to Zen practice; it is hands-on, the opposite of an intellectual endeavor. For me, as a bookworm, writer, and person who lives in her head, it has been useful to be required to do work with my hands, to make a product that needs to be done a certain way and ready at a certain time. There's no intellectualizing your way out of preparing lunch for a hundred people.

In addition to the head cook (*tenzo*) and her assistant, there were about eight kitchen apprentices — a motley crew of recovering alcoholics, twenty-somethings avoiding nine-to-five jobs, aspiring religious clergy, and people for whom these categories overlapped. We would meet every day in the *tenzo*'s office at 8:30 AM, a half an hour after breakfast ended, to read out loud a chapter from *Zen Mind, Beginner's Mind* — the famous book by Shunryu Suzuki Roshi — and discuss the menu for the day. Kitchen apprentices would volunteer for or be assigned certain tasks. Preparing the day's lunch soup was the job everyone wanted, as it was the main attraction of the day. But most of the work was prep — chopping carrots, potatoes, and onions; stripping kale; washing lettuce.

My roommate's name was Nicole, a droll low-key woman in her late twenties who had years of professional kitchen experience at an organic café. She was hooking up (millennial-speak for "having sex") with another kitchen apprentice on the down-low, which I appreciated since I was also dating a man I shouldn't have been (new relationships are forbidden during the first six months at all SFZC locations). The *tenzo* — an exhausted-looking middle-aged novelist I assumed had been thrust into the position against her will — quickly incorporated Nicole into the decision-making process of the

kitchen, giving her most of the responsibility for menu planning and actual cooking.

Over the months I worked at Green Gulch, I learned a
lot from Nicole. She taught me the importance of salt (lots
of salt), how to add dried herbs early in the cooking process
and large amounts of fresh herbs right at the end, and how to
make a good salad dressing. She worked at a steady, diligent
pace, not breaking concentration to laugh or chat until the
dish she was making was completed.

Vegetarian cooking in northern California is different
from the temple food I prepared in Japan; the vegetables, ingredients, and flavor profiles are all different. The only real
similarity is that there is no meat. At Green Gulch, most dishes
started with a base of olive oil, onions, garlic, and dried herbs,
to which the other ingredients were added. One day a week,
each kitchen apprentice was assigned to cook breakfast alone
— a formidable task that required missing morning zazen
and working straight through until breakfast. Because I had
lived in Japan for years, the *tenzo* assigned me to the weekly
Japanese-themed breakfast. It consisted of rice porridge, miso
soup, baked porridge, and oven-baked tofu.

⬤ OVEN-BAKED TOFU

Oven-Baked Tofu is adapted from the recipe used in the kitchen
at Green Gulch.

Serves 4

> 2 blocks (14 ounces each) extra-firm tofu,
>   cut into bite-size cubes
> ½ cup sesame oil
> ½ cup soy sauce

1 piece (1½ inches) ginger, peeled and finely chopped
6 green onions, thinly sliced

Marinate the tofu overnight in a mixture of the sesame oil, soy sauce, and ginger. Stir the marinade at least once, so that all sides of the tofu are equally coated.

Preheat the oven to 400°F. Spread the tofu evenly in a single layer on a baking sheet. Bake for 25 to 30 minutes. Turn the tofu once after 15 minutes and check regularly after that, turning once more if needed. The tofu is done when all sides are crispy but not burned. You may need more cooking time.

Remove the tofu from the oven, toss it with the green onions, and plate.

The first day I was assigned to cook breakfast, I dragged myself to the kitchen while it was still dark. The Green Gulch kitchen is a large half-underground basement-like room, with stoves and ovens spanning the entire far wall. In the middle of the kitchen are four large counters for chopping vegetables; utensils, measuring cups, and bowls are stored underneath.

A seasoned kitchen apprentice named Jill was tasked with teaching me the ropes of cooking breakfast. I knew my way around the kitchen, but had never prepared this specific meal for so many people, and I was practically illiterate when it came to using an oven. During the many years I lived in Japan I never encountered a single oven; ovens exist in high-end bakeries in the big cities, but that's about it. Japan is a simmering culture, I'm convinced.

I told Jill I was confident about making the rice porridge and miso soup — I'd made those hundreds of times in Japan — so she busied herself preparing the tofu and setting the table. As in Japan, I added the rice to a large pot of water. Once the water boiled, I turned down the heat to the lowest simmer possible and then turned to work on the miso soup.

I was sure everything was going well with the meal we were preparing until the *tenzo* came to check on us an hour and a half later. She asked how the porridge was doing, and I confidently lifted the lid, showing her the barely simmering pot. In Japan, rice porridge is supposed to be smooth and watery. I was always instructed to avoid stirring the pot until the very end, because stirring rice prematurely makes the dish cloudy. The goal in making rice porridge in Japan is to achieve a smooth, nearly translucent consistency.

The *tenzo* looked at my porridge and gasped.

"The rice is barely cooked!" she exclaimed. "Have you stirred it at all?"

"Nope!" I said, proud of my Japanese rice-cooking pedigree. The *tenzo* looked at the clock with exasperation.

"Breakfast is in twenty minutes, and this is barely cooked!" she said, turning up the heat full blast and reaching for a large metal spoon.

I gulped. "In Japan — !" I heard myself protest, then bit my tongue.

The *tenzo* took over the rice porridge, stirring it with fury as the water boiled. Somewhere, the God of Rice Porridge was looking down on her with wrath, I was sure. I busied myself with washing dishes and finishing the miso soup, trying to remind myself to obey the custom of the country. When in California, do as the Californians do.

I managed to avoid disaster with the pot of miso soup, although the preparation was different from what I was used to. I discovered that the "miso" at Green Gulch was not actually miso — in Japan, miso is made from soybeans, but at Green Gulch we were required to cook with chickpea miso due to the number of people (four out of several hundred) with soy allergies. This is another difference between Japanese and American communal cooking; in Japan, people will suffer (nonlethal) allergies and dislike of certain foods in silence out of fear of offending their hosts, but at Western dharma centers we go out of our way to accommodate even one person with a food preference. I am not sure which is the more compassionate way.

The chickpea "miso" was white paste. And instead of using a special miso strainer to muddle the paste in the hot water, as in Japan, the *tenzo* told me to simply put the miso in a bowl, add hot water, whisk, and add this mixture to the pot of cooked vegetables. I refrained from saying "In Japan…" this time and obeyed, not wanting to upset her any more.

We served breakfast on time — it was hot, there was enough of it, and nobody died, which is always a good measure of how a meal goes. But it had been a stressful event. From that day on I realized I would need to throw out — or at least put aside — all my Japanese techniques and learn the required recipes anew. This was a good strategy, not just for getting along with my superiors and coworkers, but also because the kitchen at Green Gulch cooked for a much larger, much pickier group of people. The ingredients, pots, and pans were different. Green Gulch is situated on an organic farm in northern California that grows an abundance of chard, kale, and lettuce — but no Japanese vegetables like burdock root and daikon. So the method of preparing food was different.

Over the next few months I perfected the "Japanese" breakfast. Breakfast turned over almost immediately into lunch, which was always salad, fresh baked bread, and a soup like cashew-tomato, lentil, or black bean. Dinner could be a variety of things — barbecued tofu, Mexican spreads, spicy sweet-potato fries, stir-fries. I learned how to roast vegetables so that they were crispy but not burned and fell in love with ovens. What amazing machines! Eventually I graduated to a different breakfast, which I came to enjoy even more than the Japanese meal: tempeh hash.

⦿ TEMPEH HASH À LA GREEN GULCH

The diverse blend of herbs — both dried and fresh — gives this dish a hearty, comforting taste. I've found that sage is really the magic ingredient, but it helps to use as many different herbs as you can.

Serves 4

> About ½ cup olive oil, *divided*
> 18 ounces tempeh (fermented soybean cake),
>   cut into ¾-inch cubes
> 1 large potato, cut into ¾-inch cubes (about 2 cups)
> ½ sweet potato or yam, cut into ¾-inch cubes
> Salt and pepper
> 1 onion, diced medium
> 3 large cloves garlic, minced
> ¾ teaspoon dried oregano
> ¾ teaspoon dried basil
> ¾ teaspoon dried sage
> ¾ teaspoon dried thyme
> 3 tablespoons chopped fresh rosemary
> 2 to 3 tablespoons chopped fresh thyme, or whatever
>   fresh herb you have on hand

Add about ¼ cup of olive oil to the tempeh and turn once to coat all sides. Marinate the tempeh overnight.

Preheat the oven to 450°F. Place the potatoes on one end of a baking sheet and the sweet potatoes on the other. Drizzle each with about 1½ tablespoons of olive oil and toss to coat. Salt and pepper the potatoes generously. Place the tempeh on a separate baking sheet (all of these will cook at different times) and salt it as well.

Put both pans into the hot oven and roast for about 25 minutes, turning once, so that the potatoes and tempeh become crispy on all sides. The sweet potatoes may cook a bit faster than the regular potatoes, but this will depend on your potatoes.

While the potatoes and tempeh are roasting, sauté the onions in 1 tablespoon of olive oil until they caramelize, about 5 minutes. Add the garlic, stir, and cook another 30 seconds. Add the roasted potatoes, sweet potatoes, tempeh, and all the dried herbs, stirring so that the herbs are evenly distributed. Continue cooking on medium-low, stirring frequently, for another 5 minutes, until the tempeh is flavored with the herbs and garlic. Turn off the heat and then add the fresh herbs and salt and pepper to taste.

There was a constant debate in the Green Gulch kitchen about double-panning. The *tenzo*, being cautious, preferred to roast everything using two baking sheets at a time to prevent burning. The *tenzo*'s assistant, being a bit more of a maverick, would roast everything on one sheet, turning the items frequently. In the beginning of my tenure cooking tempeh hash, I was afraid of burning things, so I double-panned the potatoes.

Meanwhile, I was deliriously in love. Gensan bought a car just so he could drive up to Marin on weekends to see me. He would book a guest room in Green Gulch's plush retreat center, and we would spend all my free time together, walking down to the beach through the flower gardens, fields of vegetables, and horse barns.

The first time he came to visit, he brought three different boxes of chocolate and a *New York Times* article that was going around called "To Fall in Love with Anyone, Do This," which contained a series of questions to ask to — allegedly — make your partner fall in love with you. I think that may have been the happiest day of my life: lying in bed, eating three different kinds of chocolate, asking this man intimate questions, and having him ask me questions in return.

He came to visit every week. When he came, I would sleep in his guest bedroom instead of the room I shared with Nicole. We would stay up too late talking, kissing, and generally being in love. When the wake-up bell rang the next morning while it was still dark out, I would peel myself from him and put on my priest's robe, trying not to faint from tiredness. During those mornings of predawn exhaustion, it made sense to me why Buddhist nuns are not supposed to have boyfriends. But I didn't care. I am nothing if not willful.

He let me use his car whenever I wanted. On my days off I would drive down to see him. He worked full-time at a large tech company in San Francisco, but woke up every morning before 5:00 AM to go to the meditation hall. The happiest days were the ones when I could spend two nights in a row at his place. I would sleepily watch him get ready for work, marveling at the surreality of dating someone who wore collared shirts to work every day, and then write during the day while he was gone.

At night he would come home tired, and we would order Chinese food and watch television, naked, in his bed, like lazy college students. I was already in love with him by then, but when I discovered his favorite show was *Buffy the Vampire Slayer*, it was all over for me. A kind Buddhist man with a steady job who enjoyed watching *Buffy the Vampire Slayer*? I crumbled.

Some evenings I would drive down to San Francisco after my shift ended, spend a few hours at his place, and then drive home to Green Gulch at night. Those nights were the hardest. By the time I drove home, I would already be exhausted from an early morning, a day spent working in a hot kitchen, and an hour plus of driving. The road to Green Gulch is a twisted highway that winds through high cliffs, and in the dark and fog it becomes quite precarious to drive. As I clutched the steering wheel, driving as fast as I could to get home — I had to wake up at 4:45 AM — but slow enough that I wouldn't drive over the cliffs, I began to wonder if this lifestyle was sustainable (at what point would I get so exhausted that I would fall asleep at the wheel and fall to my death?).

When I finally arrived safely, I would collapse on my bed but continue to text him for a half hour or so before falling asleep. The morning came far too soon. In the zendo at 5:00 AM I would fight off sleep — my fear of forgetting to ring the appropriate bell was the only thing keeping me awake.

When I got into graduate school, I had to decide if I would move to Los Angeles. Living at Green Gulch was starting to feel unfulfilling. I wanted a Zen teacher but didn't fully click with anyone, and if I am being honest with myself, I don't think I was in the psychological state to start a relationship with a new teacher so soon after receiving Dharma transmission. I wanted to live my own life, to understand what Buddhist practice meant in the context of work, love, and domestic life.

I kept working in the kitchen, cooking tempeh hash for breakfast once a week, until I made my decision to leave and accept a spot at the University of Southern California. Around that time, I discovered that vegetables roast a lot better on one pan than two.

"Why does anyone double-pan?" I remarked to the *tenzo*'s assistant one day. "You can't get anything crispy enough with two baking sheets. If you use one sheet on a really high temperature, you just use tons of oil and turn the potatoes a lot. Then they get crispy and delicious."

The *tenzo*'s assistant grinned. "You've learned everything I have to teach you," he murmured.

And it was true. I had learned valuable cooking lessons: that vegetables tossed in good olive oil, sprinkled generously with salt and pepper, and roasted fearlessly on high heat are one of life's great pleasures. That dried herbs need time and should be added early. That it is nearly impossible to add too many fresh herbs to a pot of soup when cooking for fifty people, but that fresh herbs are the *je ne sais quoi* that makes a dish special.

A month later, Gensan and I moved to Los Angeles. He had decided to come with me after only a few months of dating. Not everyone was happy he was coming with me. In fact, a lot of people were upset. For one thing, Gensan was ten years older than I was and a serious Zen student studying to be a priest. I was the young thing with impressive and unbelievable credentials who had floated into the institution as if I owned the place and then walked away with everyone's favorite, the most promising student. Onlookers were not sure who was taking advantage of whom but were convinced something was off. We had only been together a brief time, and his future was uncertain with me.

"This is what happens," an older priest snorted. "A promising student on a clear path of practice, and they throw it all out the window as soon as they start dating someone." The bitterness in her voice was palpable.

But I was tired of people in robes telling me what to do. One morning in July we loaded up a van early in the morning and ran away together, leaving the priests and decorum behind. If I were in Japan, I would have stayed in the monastery. I would have had some kind of restraint. But this was California, the birthplace of free love and the hippie movement. So I did as Californians do.

⦿ EVERYONE'S FAVORITE
CASHEW-TOMATO SOUP

Serves 3 to 4

1 cup raw cashews, soaked in 1 cup water for 3 hours
    or overnight
1 tablespoon olive oil
½ onion, minced
3 cloves garlic, minced
1 teaspoon dried basil
½ teaspoon dried oregano
1 can (28 ounces) diced tomatoes
1 tablespoon sugar (optional)
Salt to taste
Fresh basil, for garnish

Place the cashews and their soaking water in a blender and blend until smooth and resembling chunky milk (there can be a few small chunks of cashew).

In the olive oil on low sauté the onion until translucent, about 5 minutes. Add the garlic, basil, and oregano and continue cooking another 1 to 2 minutes. Add the canned tomatoes and bring to a boil; then simmer until the tomato sauce is heated through and slightly thickened, about 10 minutes. Add the sugar and salt to taste.

Add the blended cashew mixture to the tomato sauce. Stir until everything is incorporated. Blend two-thirds of the soup in a blender until completely smooth and there are no more chunks of tomato or cashew. Combine the blended soup with the remaining one-third of unblended soup. This creates a good consistency. Stir again, and garnish with plenty of fresh basil.

8

JUST ENOUGH BRIDEZILLA

How to Have a Modestly Blingy Wedding

Brides-to-be: your goal, if you choose to accept it, is to never utter the phrase, "It's my day" during the wedding-planning process. Or the word "perfect." Your wedding will not be perfect, and it is not your special day. For one thing, it is also your partner's day, and if you've invited your family, their day as well. The day does not belong to you alone. But it is not your day either. This double negative is an important reality to be comfortable with.

Our engagement was not romantic. I was in Japan to help with *obon*, the annual Buddhist festival to honor ancestors. *Obon* is always the busiest time of the year for Zen monks and nuns, who spend one month in the summer going from house to house — often on foot — chanting sutras at family altars. My teacher, the monk who had ordained me five years previously, had enlisted my help for the July period of intensive chanting services. Gensan had accompanied me to ask my teacher permission to marry me. If there is a less romantic premise to an engagement than a man asking an abbot for permission to marry his nun, I do not know what it is. Hopefully there is a proverb out there along the lines of, "The worse the engagement, the better the marriage."

When we arrived at Toshoji, it was the end of July, and the heat felt like a wall falling down on us. We were given separate bedrooms, according to monastery custom, and changed into *samue* (Japanese work clothes), which worsened the feeling of suffocating from heat. After moving into our rooms, I checked up on Gensan; when I saw his face, I immediately regretted inviting him. He seemed scared, hot, and overwhelmed, all of which he was. He didn't speak a word of Japanese, and as a layperson he was mostly ignored by the monks and nuns, whereas I easily fell back into the routine of monastery life. Putting on the robes, sitting zazen, chanting, and speaking Japanese were all muscle memory to me at that point.

Despite the muscle memory, it was not a smooth transition for me, though. Almost every day I ended up in tears, not sure if I belonged in this life anymore — suspecting that I had moved on to a new chapter of my life but not ready to let my nun's identity go. I fought bitterly with the abbot, who felt I was abandoning him (I was), and who I felt had hurt me too deeply for us to continue any sort of relationship (he had). Gensan went on walks with me at lunch and held me while I cried. Despite being the one who didn't speak the language and who was more physically uncomfortable, he managed to be steady and comforting. That's when I decided to marry him.

As early as a few weeks into our relationship, he had floated the idea of our getting married. Almost weekly he sent me links to articles with titles like "How Soon Is Too Soon to Get Engaged?" and "50 Questions to Ask Your Partner Before You Propose."

"I don't know, six months?" I suggested in response to his question of timing. In truth, though, I didn't know if it was too soon or not soon enough. What is the "right amount of time" to wait before getting engaged? Who decides this, and how?

After a week in the main monastery, we moved to my teacher's family temple high up in the mountains to help out with the *obon* chanting there — each temple has its own members, like a congregation, who require chanting services. I promptly became too ill to move from an infection that had never quite gone away, and I spent the rest of the trip on a futon on the floor, turning up the fan and guzzling antibiotics.

At some point, Gensan had a conversation with my teacher about our getting married. My teacher seemed enthusiastic — I couldn't help but think he was trying to get rid of me — and gave us some traditional marriage beads called *juzu* as a parting gift, along with an envelope of cash in congratulations. When we finally said good-bye to my teacher and left the monastery, we were grateful to be back in civilization. At the train station I suggested he buy me a diamond ring.

"Now?" he asked, incredulous.

"Sure," I said. "We can have an engagement conversation tonight."

"An engagement conversation?"

"Yes, like where we discuss getting married."

I didn't like the idea of being proposed to. I thought it was archaic and sexist, but I couldn't really avoid the tradition altogether. I knew I wanted a ring.

My life often approaches the conventional like this and then veers away from it, only to have fate, social conditioning, or chaos grab the wheel and steer me back on course. For example, I lost my virginity the night before prom. My boy-friend and I had both decided that losing our virginity to each other on prom night would be too cliché. So about sixteen hours before senior prom, in an awkward, unsatisfying, yet heartfelt five minutes, we narrowly escaped becoming adolescent stereotypes.

The story leading up to senior prom is just as convoluted, with me heading in one direction and changing my mind midway. I'd gone to prom the year before with friends and hated it, so I decided to skip it my senior year. Prom, after all, was a sexist social construct. But to my surprise my childhood crush asked me to go to prom with him at his school, and I said yes. Soon after, we started dating. I planned on reusing my prom dress from the year before, since I was just going to make my boyfriend happy. He went to another school anyway, so he hadn't seen it before, and do you remember the part about prom (and prom dresses) being a social construct?

A week before senior prom, I remember sitting in the car with my mom, talking to her about the dress. And then, out of nowhere, I started to cry. I didn't want to wear the same dress twice. I was in love, and it was prom, and it wouldn't be special if I wore the dress again. My mom looked at me, smiled, and without missing a beat said, "Well, let's go get you a dress then!" We went to the nearest dress store and bought a fancy cocktail dress. Even rebels want to look good at prom.

Gensan did buy a ring, but he had put a credit limit on his card before the trip, and so it was a small diamond ring. We planned a dinner at a fancy restaurant at the top of a sky-scraper in Tokyo. He had the new diamond ring, and I had the *juzu* beads. I used the congratulations money my teacher had given me to buy a new dress. I have to imagine that using money from the abbot who ordains you to buy a dress for your engagement must be the equivalent, karmically, of sell-ing your daughter's favorite toy to buy drugs, but I was in full

California mode at that point — patriarchy and propriety be damned! I was also proud of myself for approaching my engagement with such maturity. We were just two adults having a conversation about their future.

As soon as we set foot in the restaurant, I knew we had made a miscalculation. There was a grand piano in the center of the restaurant, where a man was plunking away at sappy American love songs. The restaurant itself was on the fifteenth floor of a fancy hotel, and although the view was quite lovely, the exaggerated heart decor on the tables and neon lights on the walls made the whole space seem more like a Disneyland ride called Tokyo Engagement Mountain.

Gensan was confused about what I was asking for. I had told him I wanted our engagement to be a mature conversation between two adults (I believe I had explicitly said, "No grand gestures, no getting down on one knee"), but as I sat on Tokyo Engagement Mountain, my social conditioning kicked in and I grew resentful and impatient, waiting for the romance. Where was my grand gesture? Why wasn't he getting down on one knee? While picking at our $200 Japanese-European fusion prix-fixe meal, we had an excruciatingly painful conversation that went nowhere. We left before dessert was even served, frustrated and tired. Back in the hotel room he managed to get down on one knee, finally, but it was too little too late. I felt unwanted, as though he had copped out.

It was only years later that I realized Gensan had only been doing what I explicitly asked. This was difficult for me to understand: a man, doing what I asked? Listening to me? Impossible! But I learned my lesson. I was marrying someone who listened to the words I said and respected them.

When we told my parents we were engaged, I informed them I wanted to hold the wedding in the backyard and order Chinese takeout for the reception. Thankfully, they did not entertain this idea for very long. Eventually my father offered to pay for the wedding in exchange for inviting his whole extended family. It was an offer we couldn't refuse.

As the wedding plans progressed, I struggled, like most brides-to-be, with my mother's expectations. Adding parents and money to the ingredient list of a wedding changes things. Once parents have a stake in the wedding, it is no longer about you and your partner celebrating your love and commitment, but about family as well. A wedding is about two people making a lifetime commitment, but it is an important moment for parents and family to come together and celebrate a communal milestone. This is the major way a wedding isn't entirely about you; it's not your special day, because it's also your mother and father's day, not to mention your husband's (or wife's) day. For my mother and father, we all knew this was probably the only chance they would get to see one of their children get married, since my brother is antimarriage and my half sister eloped without a ceremony.

I didn't always take this all in stride. Sometimes I felt as though the wedding train had gotten out of control and was speeding toward something I could neither control nor relate to. "This is just a glorified family reunion," I complained bitterly to Gensan one day when I felt overwhelmed by my mother's demands to plan things a certain way. I was resisting very basic things like buying flowers, wearing a white dress, planning a father-daughter dance, and having special colors for the reception.

"We need to pick colors for the wedding party and reception," she had informed me matter-of-factly over the phone.

"No colors," I insisted. "I only have one bridesmaid, and she's wearing blue. Gensan's best man is his sister. Why do we need colors?"

My mother did not have an answer for that.

There were many things I deemed unnecessary — having a DJ, wearing a garter, assigning seating at the reception — but

other traditions I felt more conflicted about. A woman does not abandon the custom of wearing a white dress at a wedding lightly. I don't say this out of some bullshit sexist notion of how things *should* be at a wedding. There are no shoulds. No one needs to wear a white dress. People get married in Star Wars gear, and if that works for them, that's great.

But a wedding is a ceremony, and a ceremony is made up of symbols working together to create meaning. The goal of a wedding is to make you feel married at the end, and these various traditions help us feel something special is taking place. I have practiced as a Zen priest for long enough to know the power of symbol and ceremony. A successful ceremony has symbols and tools, and the wedding dress is one such symbol.

In the end, I'm happy with how things turned out. Our "rehearsal dinner" was in my parents' dining room, just twelve of our closest friends and family. My father, Tony, cooked for hours and made the lemon sorbet "cups" he makes on Thanksgiving and Christmas, hollowed-out lemons filled with the icy sweet dessert. There was prosecco and no stress.

⦿ TONY'S LEMON SORBET

Try to choose lemons with a flat bottom. This will facilitate their staying upright in the baking pan.

Makes 12 lemon "cups"

>   12 to 14 lemons (Meyer lemons are best)
>   1½ cups fresh lemon juice
>   2 cups water
>   2 cups extra-fine sugar

Cut off the top third of 12 of the lemons. Over a bowl, use a spoon to scrape out the lemon pulp. Squeeze the juice from the pulp. If you have more than 1½ cups, use the extra juice for another purpose. If you do not have 1½ cups, you may need to juice additional lemons to get sufficient juice. Refrigerate the lemon "cups" until ready to use.

Combine the water and sugar in a heavy saucepan, bring to a boil, and cook until the sugar is dissolved, about 1 minute. Add the lemon juice and stir well. Cool the mixture to room temperature and then place it in the refrigerator to chill. Freeze the mixture in an ice-cream maker (it will not become fully hard), spoon it into the prepared lemon "cups," place them in a flat baking pan or pie pan, and place the pan in the freezer until the desired hardness is achieved. If you don't have an ice-cream maker, pour the liquid into a flat baking pan and place it in the freezer. Stir it every 15 or 20 minutes until frozen into a slush and then fill the lemon cups with it.

If made ahead of time, let the cups sit at room temperature until the sorbet softens to the desired consistency.

I did find a discounted white dress that I loved. And somewhere along the line, Gensan and I decided to have two ceremonies — a traditional Zen Buddhist ceremony held at San Francisco Zen Center on Friday and a white-dress ceremony the next day in Golden Gate Park followed by a boozy reception. Consulting with our officiant, we found out that it is quite common for interracial or bicultural couples to have two ceremonies. The nun side of me needed to have her solemn day.

But the California girl was there too. I have heard people say their wedding was the best day of their life, and I was not expecting that at all. But I think it may have been the best day of my life. Or, if I'm being honest, definitely within the top five. I was surrounded by loved ones, celebrating a mysterious and wonderful love I had stumbled upon.

Gensan and I both cried almost the whole way through the ceremony. At the reception, my mother surprised me by organizing my cousins to play an Irish wedding song I had loved as a child. This was followed by a champagne tower (my idea, clearly). There was no bouquet toss, no father-daughter dance, no assigned seating. The dinner was casual but elegant. I wore a faux leather jacket over my white dress, and my husband painted his nails blue to match his blue tuxedo.

By the end of the night he ended up with a flower crown on his head. There was an open bar, and we danced to a mix my cousin had made on his iPhone. The last event of the night was a piñata, which I barely remember hitting. Nor do I remember stuffing candy down my brassiere in gleeful exhilaration and abandon — though photographic evidence exists.

We exchanged new rings. One of the hardest parts of the wedding-planning process was grappling with the fact that I disliked my engagement ring. The engagement had been such a mess, the ring purchased on the fly. It was a small diamond on a plain silver band. I wanted to remedy that, but I felt guilty about wanting a larger diamond. I have a severe allergy to women posting Instagram photos of their engagement rings, and I wanted to avoid being the kind of woman who stresses about the size of the engagement diamond. I don't think money buys love or proves love.

After years of being a nun and working to end my desire for worldly things, I couldn't justify to myself wanting a more expensive ring. Yet I couldn't help what I was feeling — call it social conditioning, greed, or just having standards. I knew the ring was something I wanted to wear forever.

What do you do with a feeling of greed you can't get rid of? Feelings cannot be thrown away, but at the same time, they are empty of inherent existence. They both are and are not real, like a rainbow.

After months of feeling guilty ("materialistic" and "greedy" were some of the insults I flung at myself), I finally discussed this with Gensan. Once it was out in the open, I felt better about it. He didn't judge me for wanting a better ring, and I agreed to split the cost with him. We found a jeweler who proposed resetting the initial diamond in a larger ring.

"I don't need or want superbling," I told the jeweler.

She was used to this kind of conversation, and undaunted. "Sure, but with your personality, you need something more… dramatic," she said diplomatically.

Later, when I saw the end result, I smiled. She had set the initial diamond into a ring of smaller diamonds, like a flower.

"It's still modest," she explained.

I laughed. The new ring was costing us thousands of dollars. "Oh, I don't think this is *modest*."

"Okay, it's modestly blingy."

And it was.

There is a middle way for everything. It just depends on how far to the left or right you start.

9

RAMEN

Tracing a Favorite Meal across Continents

Like most Americans growing up in the 1990s, I first encountered ramen in the packaged form. It was either Maruchan or Nissin brand, the plastic packages containing blocks of noodles that you boil for three minutes and add a flavor packet. My father would scramble an egg into the boiling water with a fork, so there were chunks of soft, pillowy egg floating in the broth, turning everything yellow. It was hot and salty and delicious.

My parents were weird, former radical hippies turned wealthy medical professionals. They cared about health. They prioritized vegetables. I went in for a yearly checkup at Kaiser (my parents were employees), and my mother proudly informed the pediatrician: "We make an effort to eat vegetables with every meal." This may have been an exaggeration, as I distinctly remember licking the cream cheese off of bagels and leaving it at that.

My father was kind and quiet, better at cooking than my mother, which set an unattainably high bar for future men in my life. He made Italian pasta with sausages and chicken simmered in tomato sauce, orange sorbet served in hollowed-out tangerine skin cups. He bottled his own raspberry-infused vinegar and made homemade jam. I am not sure how Top Ramen made its way into this equation. Maybe he was tired. Perhaps the inclusion of an egg — protein — negated the artificial, nutritionless quality of the ramen. (This is often my mother's excuse for eating junk food. "Peanuts have protein!" she'll say to justify a Snickers.)

But then again, my parents' thinking about food, health, and well-being did not follow a clear logic. For example, I was not allowed to carry my lunch to school in a plastic lunch box — they gave me a straw basket — yet we ate at Burger King once a month. They would not let me watch television or eat Pop-Tarts or Froot Loops, yet the freezer was stocked with frozen dinners. I was prohibited from eating food that came in Styrofoam for environmental concerns, but we owned two cars and flew on airplanes frequently.

When I was ten, I was old enough to know when things were not fair. Of course, I could only see when things were not fair *for me*; I was blissfully unaware of anything like race or class privilege, of which I had an abundance. My mother packed my lunch every day (in the above-mentioned straw basket). They were fairly balanced lunches: a turkey sandwich on the kind of fancy, seed-topped baguette that years later I cannot justify purchasing on my writer's budget, with mayonnaise and cranberry sauce, a crunchy homage to Thanksgiving leftovers. Other days I would have a bagel and cream cheese, or if I was very lucky, cucumber sushi from the local gourmet grocery store. Each lunch contained an apple or orange or sometimes multiple fruits. There was very little artificial anything, although Doritos made it in there sometimes. More inconsistency!

Some of my classmates had Cup Noodles for lunch. This was similar to the ramen my parents made me, but came in a Styrofoam cup; you poured boiling water into it and it was ready to eat after three minutes. I'm not sure how I got my hands on my first Cup Noodles, but at some point I ate them, and they were everything my own lunches were not: salty, carbohydrate-centric, bursting with MSG, devoid of any kind of fruit or vegetables. I wanted my own Cup Noodles for lunch the same way I wanted a plastic lunch box instead of a damn straw basket — the same way I wanted Barbie dolls but was given silk scarves and pine cones to play with (I kid you not).

True to form, they refused my request for Cup Noodles (remember, no Styrofoam). I begged. They explained their reasoning: the immortality of Styrofoam, corporate greed, and the degradation of Mother Earth. They suggested I write to the makers of Cup Noodles and ask them to start using paper cups instead. To prove their point that Styrofoam is unnecessary, my parents bought me organic Cup Noodle knockoffs that came in paper cups. The taste of the organic broth was so terrible I threw it out after one spoonful.

Perhaps my entire childhood could be characterized as a battle with my parents to get them to let me enjoy plastic products and artificially flavored food. I have no memory of my older brother arguing for artificially flavored food, but we

did sneak in some television when my parents were out, turning it off and running out of the room as soon as we heard the garage door open.

With no other recourse, and filled with an obsessive craving for instant chemical noodles I could make at school, I wrote to the makers of Cup Noodles. This was before we owned a computer, so I wrote the letter out by hand, in the scrawl of a ten-year-old. I put it in an envelope and mailed it. A few weeks later I received a response. It was typed and cordial, thanking me for my love of Cup Noodles and regretfully informing me that they could not use paper cups in lieu of Styrofoam, something about cost effectiveness and business practices, blah blah blah.

Enclosed in their letter was a coupon for two free Cup Noodles. I asked my parents if I could use the coupons, and they said yes, I'd earned it. I ran to the corner store and breathlessly redeemed my two free Cup Noodles (this was the moment I learned, erroneously, that political activism is an enjoyable activity that yields immediately satisfying results). I did not think to ask my parents why redeeming my coupons for two free Styrofoam Cup Noodles was better than buying them, because my mouth was too full of glorious, artificially flavored instant noodles to talk.

At the age of twenty-eight I found a job with a study-abroad program in Kyoto. I applied to it while still living at Nisodo, on my laptop using Starbucks public Wi-Fi when I was supposed to be grocery shopping. Miraculously, I got the job without even having an interview. A month later, after five years in the monastic system, I walked out the door.

The students in the study-abroad program and I stayed in an inn around the block from Higashi Honganji, the main Pure Land Buddhist temple in Kyoto. We were given the equivalent of $20 a day as a food stipend, which, we quickly realized, does not go a long way if you don't have a kitchen. But there were noodle shops. For around $7 you could get a large bowl of udon, soba, or ramen.

Above the Kyoto train station was an entire floor of ramen shops. Dozens and dozens of ramen stalls, all collected in one place in one massive mall. It got crowded around mealtime, but it was always possible to find one shop with fewer people. At each place you ordered off a touch screen, choosing the exact meal combination you wanted and putting cash into the device. Once you sat down, you handed the ticket to the server, who disappeared into the kitchen and returned five minutes later with your food.

The broth was hot and salty. After so many years of rice gruel, the richness of the fat and salt felt like a slap in the face, but the good kind of slap, like a friend at a bar screaming, "Pull yourself together, man!" before taking your car keys. The ramen was nothing like what I'd eaten in America. The noodles were firmer, wider, and chewier. The broth tasted like, well, actual broth, and there was a healthy dollop of sautéed vegetables on top in addition to egg and ham. I was surprised and delighted by how many *things* were in it. It was like a whole city.

At one point I wandered into a ramen shop two blocks away from our inn, where I easily ordered off the picture menu. It was less crowded than the shops above the train station, just a small place along the main drag. It had no tables, just one long counter around the cash register with stools for sitting, like a bar. Over the next few months I ate there about once or twice a week, sampling everything — the *gyoza* that came neatly fried in one nearly singular sheet, fried rice and beer, and all the flavors of ramen that were offered.

At the shop I saw families eating with children and young people on dates, but more often than not, I saw businessmen eating alone, still wearing their white collared shirts from work. Half the people in there always seemed sad and lonely, which was fine by me because so was I. I was a refugee nun on the run, trying to forge a new relationship to society, wearing normal clothes for the first time in years. I was tall and bald and foreign, but I didn't feel out of place at the ramen shop. It was a place you go to eat cheap, salty, satisfying food in under fifteen minutes, not talking to anyone, before you go home to watch TV alone.

⬤ CHILLED RAMEN (*HIYASHI CHUKA*)

At some point during the summer, usually in June, *hiyashi chuka* appears in noodle shops across Japan. The same way cherry blossoms signify spring, *hiyashi chuka* means that hot weather has arrived. *Hiyashi chuka* refers to a cold ramen dish with a variety of toppings and a cold sweet vinegar broth often seasoned with hot mustard or chili oil (*hiyashi* means "cold" or "chilled," and *chuka* means "Chinese food").

In noodle shops the dish comes topped with a variety of vegetables, sliced ham, and egg — either hard-boiled or fried as a thin omelet and sliced into strips — but it is still delicious served without ham and eggs. At Nisodo we would substitute sliced stewed shiitake mushrooms for the ham, but to be honest, shiitake and ham are quite different tastes, and ham tastes far subtler than the earthy shiitakes. Feel free to mix and match the toppings to your liking; the broth is delicious enough that almost any combination of toppings is great! The point of this dish is to cool you down on a hot day, and after one slurp of the cold tangy broth, I'm sure you'll agree it does the trick.

This dish is usually made with fresh ramen noodles, although it is actually delicious with any noodle. You could substitute dried udon if you cannot find fresh ramen. You could also use dried ramen, but udon is probably preferable.

Serves 2

2 cups *moyashi* (bean sprouts)
2 large dried shiitake mushrooms soaked overnight
   in enough water to cover
½ cup dashi
1 tablespoon sugar
1 tablespoon soy sauce
1 small cucumber, julienned
½ large tomato, cut into thin wedges, or ½ cup cherry
   tomatoes
250 grams (about 9 ounces) fresh ramen noodles
   (about 2 packets), or 200 grams (about 7 ounces)
   dried udon
Chili oil (optional)
Japanese mustard (optional)
Beni shoga (pickled red ginger; optional)

Dressing

⅓ cup soy sauce
1 tablespoon sugar
3 tablespoons rice vinegar
1½ tablespoons sesame oil
1 cup water

Blanch the *moyashi* in salted water for 2 minutes and then rinse with cold water to prevent further cooking. When cool, vigorously squeeze out any excess water with your hands.

Remove the shiitakes from the soaking liquid and slice them as thinly as you can into strips. In a saucepan bring the dashi, sugar, and soy sauce to a boil and add the shiitakes. Cook on medium for 5 minutes or until tender (watch it carefully, as the broth may suddenly caramelize, leaving the mushrooms to burn!).

Arrange the *moyashi*, mushrooms, cucumbers, and tomatoes on a plate or cutting board so they are easily accessible.
For the dressing, mix the soy sauce, sugar, vinegar, sesame oil,
and water in a bowl until the sugar has dissolved. Cook the
noodles according to package directions. Drain and rinse thoroughly with cold water to stop the cooking.

Divide the noodles into two bowls. Using your hands, carefully place the vegetables on top of the noodles in separate
areas, not touching each other. Pour the dressing over the noodles and serve with chili oil, mustard, and pickled red ginger, if
desired.

In the summer of 2016, after Gensan and I left the Bay Area, we
moved into an apartment in the neighborhood of Koreatown
in Los Angeles, so that I could pursue a master's degree in East
Asian Studies at the University of Southern California. I chose
to live in Koreatown because it was close to school — and
because the signs were not in English. It felt more like home
than a neighborhood with all its signs in English. I could easily
walk to an Asian market that sold miso, *konbu*, frozen dumplings, kimchi, and about five hundred kinds of instant ramen.
Waiting in line at the Korean supermarket while the cashiers
spoke to each other in Spanish, I wondered, not for the first
time, why I always chose to put myself in situations where I
feel out of place.

Gensan and I settled into domestic life. We bought dogs,
started a Zen sitting group in our living room, streamed Net-
flix shows, and got married. We honeymooned in Italy, eating
pizza and gelato in Venice and a smaller resort town in the
north. A few weeks after returning from the honeymoon, in
the midst of my penultimate semester at graduate school, I
came down with a bout of exhaustion so intense I could barely
lift my head. Dark circles formed under my eyes, my home-
work remained unfinished, and professors stopped me after
class to ask if I was okay. It took several more weeks before I

went to my doctor. She tested me for anemia and digestive disorders, but after the results came back negative, she informed me that I was suffering a depressive episode.

I felt not a small amount of shame about being diagnosed with depression after returning, triumphant, from a spiritual journey on the other side of the world. I was doing all the right things: getting married, working on career, practicing meditation, exercising, eating right, going to therapy. I had written and published a book and was beginning to teach Buddhism at a community in Long Beach. I was madly in love with my husband and doing work I had chosen to do. How could I be depressed?

But the more I thought about it, the more the depression made sense. Perhaps it was the comedown after a whirlwind romance, my body and mind recovering from the shock of so much change so quickly. I hated Los Angeles. It was big and dirty and impossible to get around by bus. The female college students I taught were thin and wore bright white sneakers. On a semiregular basis I had to contend with women who tried to convince me that a juice cleanse was a good idea.

I had also discovered that I disliked the academic study of Buddhism, and so graduate school was, if not torture, then at least two years of constant boredom. I spent hours upon hours translating difficult passages in Japanese and Chinese and straining my brain to read hundreds of pages of uninteresting Japanese history. After five years of living as a nun, working in community and sleeping side by side with other nuns, the academic study of Japanese Buddhism seemed so hollow, so disconnected from the lived experience of temple life.

As ever, food was my anchor. On weekends I wandered through Little Tokyo, nostalgic and bewildered, searching for ramen. I quickly realized that ramen is a hip food in Los Angeles, not a food for sad, lonely people looking to eat a quick dinner before returning to their tiny bachelor apartment. A popular ramen shop, Daikokuya, always had at least twenty people waiting outside every time I drove past it. I have an instinctual dislike of waiting in line for food I love, so I never tried to get inside. Instead, I discovered another location on the west side of Los Angeles with absolutely no line. The ramen was fine. It tasted like what I had eaten countless times in Japan. Eventually I realized that the best ramen in America tastes like average ramen in Japan.

As a master's candidate in East Asian studies, I took a required seminar on the geopolitics of China, Korea, and Japan. One of the books we read was *Rise of a Japanese Chinatown*, by Eric Han, a historical account of the development of Yokohama's Chinatown. Yokohama, a popular shipping destination in Japan, became known for Chinese immigrants, prostitution, and gambling as well as the introduction of *shumai* (Chinese dumplings) and ramen.

Han attempts to argue that in Yokohama there was no sense of being both "Chinese" and "Japanese" simultaneously; Yokohama's Chinatown was an example of a hybrid, transnational community because its inhabitants identified mainly as *local residents* rather than as Chinese or Japanese. Chinese immigrants developed both *shumai* and ramen, the latter of which quickly became a staple of Japanese food, which helped the country define and solidify its (Japanese) national identity. Han writes that the emergence of "Chinese food" as a popular staple in Japan in turn had the effect of reifying notions of Japaneseness and Japanese food. He writes, "Japan's multicultural gastronomy helped nurture a modern mass society with a new consciousness of Japan's place in the world."

I could not tell if ramen was even Japanese food in America. I wanted it to be. It often had the same ingredients, and I sought it out when I craved Japanese flavors. But the experience of eating in ramen restaurants with bars and DJs left me frustrated with the way Los Angeles hipness consumes everything good and pure in the world and converts it into a stylish product devoid of its former personality. Still, my nostalgia and obsession compelled me to keep searching for good Japanese food. I frequented Japanese restaurants, haunted Asian grocery stores, pitched a Japanese cookbook, and made elaborate vegetarian meals. These meals were something I could create on my own terms, in my own house, reminding me of what I love and what I left behind. I discovered that the ramen sold in the refrigerated section in Asian markets tastes nearly like Japanese ramen without the two-hour wait.

In the Zen tradition they speak of "stepping off a hundred-foot pole." This is a metaphor for letting go of all preconceptions and habits and embracing reality in all its terrifying newness. Researching how to make ramen from scratch, I encountered the book *Ivan Ramen*, by Ivan Orkin. He describes his frustration in developing his own unique ramen broth. After discussing his failed *tare* (concentrated stock) with his wife, he realizes:

> If I wanted to make a bowl of ramen that was personal to me, I had to approach it like any other dish I'd made. Good cooking is good cooking, regardless of whether it's Japanese or American or Puerto Rican. I put aside everything I knew about ramen save for a loose outline; then I fiddled, and read, and ate lots of noodles and lots of French, Spanish, and classical Japanese dishes.

After throwing away his preconceptions about ramen, he adapts a Spanish and Italian technique for *sofrito* — "small diced aromatics simmered slowly in oil" — to use as the foundation of his soup base.

Reading this, I realized my life was in a similar place. I had spent enough time in Japan forming my adult personality that I was having trouble letting go of that part of my life. I needed to create my own recipe — my own life — but was too attached to the Japanese way I had been taught. Part of me still felt guilty for leaving my nun's life behind; self-criticism roared in my head, hurling insults like "spoiled," "phony," and "quitter." I was afraid to let go and live fully in my American life, as my own person, but I couldn't bear the thought of returning to monastic life in Japan. And so I had been clinging to Japanese culture and Japanese food as a way of making sense of things.

I am struck by the similarities between master chefs and Buddhist masters. Both need to be apprentices, to faithfully study tradition, before they can transcend it. Moving beyond tradition is terrifying. It feels like stepping off a hundred-foot pole. Making ramen from scratch, I realized I wasn't there yet, that I hadn't developed my own fully formed and unique expression of myself. But I could sense it on the horizon.

In writings and public talks, I started taking more risks. I began stating my own opinion, my own ideas. After so many years of being taught to follow, this was terrifying. The more I articulated my own thoughts, the more I realized it wasn't a clear-cut dichotomy between tradition and secularism, between being an apprentice and acting like a maverick. I was somewhere in between — not an entirely unique, autonomous personality, but a composite of all the experiences before me, all the people I'd loved and hurt, all the people who taught me how to cook, sit, listen, and work.

Then somehow I was no longer falling off the hundred-foot pole, but flying.

It is not difficult to make good ramen. It is helpful if you can find fresh ramen, such as Sun Noodle. But fresh ramen can be found all over the country, because this is the twenty-first century and nothing is exotic anymore. I checked the Sun Noodle website, and there is even a store that carries Sun Noodle in

Overland Park, Kansas (at the unfortunately named Oriental Supermarket), and one in Memphis, Tennessee. Sun Noodle packets contain noodles and flavor pouches, which are fine, or you can make your own broth.

But, especially if you are buying fresh noodles, it is easy to make a bowl of ramen that is satisfying, feels like real food, and doesn't come from a Styrofoam cup. Chop up your favorite vegetables (I like cabbage, onions, carrots, and maybe some mushrooms) and sauté them in oil; add dashi powder and a tiny bit of soy sauce or use kimchi. If you're not feeling up for the more involved recipe, just use the flavoring pouch that comes with the fresh ramen — it's a far cry from the seasoning packets of days gone by, and it tastes good, which is the whole point.

If you want a more hands-on experience and a project that will take nearly half a day, you can create your own *tare*, or concentrated stock. This is somewhat time-consuming, but it produces really tasty soup.

● SPICY VEGAN MISO RAMEN

Spicy Vegan Miso Ramen is adapted from other recipes I have read online and in books (especially *Ramen at Home*, by Brian MacDuckston, as well as *Ivan Ramen* for general techniques) and incorporates the advice I have received from Japanese nuns on making good vegetarian stock. It's not an entirely unique recipe, but it includes elements that I uniquely enjoy eating and is the best way I know to make the dish.

Ramen *tare* in restaurants is usually made by simmering meat bones. The vegan version I have created involves simmering a veritable witches' brew of *konbu*, shiitakes, soybeans, aromatics, soy sauce, and salt (be wary, it stinks up the house!) to create a rich, salty broth. It's best to make a large quantity of soy *tare* and store it, so you do not have to recreate it from scratch each time you want ramen.

Part 1: Witches' Brew (Soy *Tare*)

Makes about 5 cups

> 10 medium dried shiitake mushrooms
> 1 ounce *konbu* (dried kelp; about 1 cup when
>   cut into 1-inch squares)
> 5 cups water
> ½ cup soybeans
> ⅔ cup soy sauce
> ⅓ cup sake
> ⅓ cup mirin
> 2 tablespoons roughly chopped green onions
> 1 tablespoon minced garlic
> 1 tablespoon minced ginger
> 2 tablespoons salt

Grind the dried shiitakes to a fine powder in a food processor. (You can also mince them very finely if you do not have a food processor.) Add the *konbu* and powdered shiitakes to the water and bring to a boil on very low heat.

In a small dry pan on medium-low, toast the soybeans until their aroma emerges, about 4 minutes (be careful not to burn them). To the shiitake-*konbu* broth add the toasted soybeans, soy sauce, sake, mirin, green onions, garlic, and ginger and simmer, stirring occasionally, for 30 minutes. Turn off the heat and let rest for another 10 to 15 minutes until it is cool enough to handle.

Remove the *konbu* and larger ingredients with tongs. Next, using a coffee filter or very fine colander, strain the liquid to remove all small particles. Stir the salt into the strained liquid.

Part 2: Spicy Miso *Tare*

Makes 1¼ cups

2 tablespoons minced garlic
2 tablespoons minced ginger
2 tablespoons chopped green onions
1 teaspoon sesame oil
1 cup red miso (or half red and half white, if you have it)
½ cup Soy *Tare* (p. 136)
⅓ cup *toban-djan* (spicy Asian fermented bean paste; the Asian sauce brand Lee Kum Kee sells this under the name "Chili Bean Sauce")
1 tablespoon sugar

In a medium pan sauté the garlic, ginger, and green onions in the sesame oil on medium-low for 1 to 2 minutes, stirring. Add the red miso, Soy *Tare*, *toban-djan*, and sugar. Lower the heat and simmer, stirring constantly, until all the ingredients are incorporated and the sauce thickens to a paste, about 3 minutes.

Part 3: Tofu "Pork"

Serves 2 to 3

1 block (14 ounces) extra-firm tofu
1 tablespoon cornstarch
Salt and pepper
1 teaspoon sesame oil

2 tablespoons minced garlic

2 tablespoons minced ginger

2 green onions, minced

3 tablespoons chopped fresh mushrooms, such as
    shiitake

1 tablespoon vegetable oil

3 teaspoons soy sauce

3 teaspoons mirin

1 teaspoon *toban-djan* (spicy fermented bean paste)

2 teaspoons sesame seeds

Cut the tofu into 1-inch-thick slices. Wrap them in paper towels, cover with a cutting board, put a weight on the board, and let sit for 30 minutes to press out excess water. In a bowl, crumble the tofu with your hands and sprinkle the cornstarch over the tofu until it is coated. Season with salt and pepper.

Heat the sesame oil in a medium frying pan and sauté the garlic, ginger, and green onions for 1 to 2 minutes. Add the mushrooms and cook another minute. Add the vegetable oil and then the coated tofu crumbles to the pan and sauté on medium-high, stirring frequently, until the tofu is brown and crispy and the mushrooms are cooked through, about 5 minutes. Add the soy sauce, mirin, and *toban-djan* and continue cooking until the liquid is absorbed into the tofu. Remove the pan from the heat and top the dish with sesame seeds.

Part 4: Spicy Miso Ramen

Serves 2 hungry people or 3 polite ones

5 cups *konbu* (dried kelp) dashi or other Japanese broth

¾ cup Spicy Miso *Tare* (p. 137)

⅓ cup tahini

1½ cups shredded cabbage

1 cup *moyashi* (bean sprouts)
1 package (12 ounces) Sun Noodle ramen (or other
   fresh ramen that serves 2 people)
1 teaspoon to 1 tablespoon chili oil
2 servings Tofu "Pork" (p. 137)
3 tablespoons sliced green onions, for garnish

Bring the *konbu* dashi to a boil in a medium saucepan. Reduce the heat to low and add the Spicy Miso *Tare* and tahini. Stir until dissolved and continue cooking another 20 minutes.

Blanch the cabbage and *moyashi* in salted water (in separate pots, if possible) for 2 minutes and then rinse under cold water to stop the cooking. Gently squeeze the vegetables to remove excess water.

Cook the noodles according to the package directions. To each serving bowl, add a small amount of chili oil, depending on how spicy you like it (1 teaspoon is enough for me, but fans of spice may want to up it to 1 tablespoon). Ladle the spicy miso broth into the bowls. Add the noodles to the broth; top them with the Tofu "Pork," cabbage, and bean sprouts; and garnish with green onions.

Variation: If you want a middle way between the quick and time-intensive methods, you can just make the Spicy Miso *Tare* (p. 137) and stir in 1 tablespoon of dashi powder in lieu of the Soy *Tare*. Add this miso mixture to the broth and complete the recipe as above.

At some point, you'll have to choose your own way. This is true in all areas of your life. Be a faithful apprentice and then take what you know into the world. With the right recipe, life is delicious. It is not perfect or instant, but it will be something you will want to eat more of.

IO

BENTO

Musings on Gender, Food, and Domesticity

Being a wife is odd. For one thing, the word *wife* is strange. It rhymes with *knife* and *strife*, perhaps uncoincidentally. The only word more strange than *wife* is *husband*, which rhymes with nothing. For months after getting married, I could not say either of these words out loud.

Before I got married, I didn't know what being a wife meant. In fact, I am still trying to figure it out. Certainly, a wife is different from a domestic partner or a live-in girlfriend — otherwise, why would the word be different? Yet for me, as a millennial steeped in feminist literature and activism who wished to carve out an identity free from gender roles, there was no clear definition of what it meant to be a wife or to have a husband beyond tax breaks. Having spent my childhood witnessing my progressive hippie parents divide household responsibilities fairly evenly, followed by a young adulthood in the most traditional religious communities in Japan, I was deeply perplexed about gender roles within marriage.

When I am in a place of discomfort or uncertainty, I rely on food. Food is my way of making sense of the world, of creating very tangible meaning with my hands. And it tastes good. Leading up to my marriage, I found myself in a full-on bento obsession — in part, I think, to try and figure out who I wanted to be as a wife. Being a woman has always confused me, and I was never more confused than during the time leading up to my marriage.

I had first encountered bento, lunches sold in colorful, neatly compartmentalized boxes, on my first visit to Japan. They are ubiquitous in train stations and sell in even the most modest of corner stores, where you can by a bento of rice, fish, and vegetables for under $5.

Before I was ordained as a nun, I learned that mothers in Japan usually craft immaculately designed bento for their children, often in the shape of children's cartoon characters or fun animals. In the photos in recipe books and on blogs, you can see meticulously crafted designs, rice balls in the shape of famous anime characters, and mini sausages made out to look like actual wiener dogs. This style of bento is called *kyaraben*, or character bento, and perusing pictures of these amazing bento is a great way to feel bad about yourself and your cooking ability! But *kyaraben* are just one kind of bento. At their most fundamental, bento boxes are just a way to carry a meal consisting of a few different items; originally bento simply consisted of rice balls and a pickle wrapped in bamboo leaves.

Women in Japan often make bento for their husbands as well as their children. For a Japanese woman, making bento is a way of not only expressing love but also demonstrating her prowess and status as a woman, since the role of a woman in Japanese society is to be a good wife, mother, and cook.

When discussing food and gender, it is impossible to ignore the special place our mother's cooking holds in our hearts. Our first food usually comes from our mother. My father was a fantastic cook, perhaps even better than my mother, but when I am sick I crave my mother's chocolate-chip cookies and noodle soup.

The best cooks I have encountered in my life have been women. In Japan, I learned to cook from nuns, most of whom had been wives and mothers before entering the monastery. For them, food was intimately connected to love and family. Making food was an act of love. On the episode "Home Cooking" on his show *Ugly Delicious*, the chef David Chang accurately noted that the ultimate goal of cooking and eating, for both men and women, is food approximating your own mother's cooking: "When you eat a dish that's not even like roast chicken," he said, "but it reminds you of roast chicken cooked by your mom, that's where you want to be at with cooking....It has less to do with perfection than with intent. The intent is more perfect."

Love by itself does not make a meal great. Too many other factors are involved — knife skills, knowledge of ingredients, technique, timing, and exactly the right amount of salt. But a truly great meal cannot be made without love.

The best cook I met in Japan was named Chuho-san. She was not a professional chef, but a nun. (Women chefs in Japan are rare; someone once told me this is because people believe women's hands are "too hot." Clearly, gender discrimination in professional cooking exists in the West too.) However, she was not a Zen master either. In fact, she was ordained about two years after I was and was essentially a novice when I met her. Before becoming a nun, she had lived a full, busy life as a wife and mother. Like many Japanese nuns these days, she entered monastic life only after raising her children and reaching the end of her responsibilities to her family in middle age.

Working together in the kitchen at the convent, she once told me that in her former life as a layperson she would wake up at 5:00 AM every day to make bento lunches for her husband and children, cook them all breakfast, go to work, and then come home from work and cook dinner. Unfortunately for the ghost of Betty Friedan, this schedule is common for Japanese wives, as even preschools enforce the expectation that mothers will make bento for their children.

Because of the many years spent cooking meals while juggling family responsibilities and her own work, Chuho-san's meals were always incredible. They were delicate in flavor but rich and satisfying, the vegetables chopped meticulously and the side dishes arranged beautifully. In fact, when I didn't know who exactly had cooked the day's meal, I could always tell when it was Chuho-san.

When you live, work, and bathe together with the same women for years, as we did at the convent, a strange thing happens. You learn to know who is approaching you from down the hallway by their footsteps and to recognize who cooked which dish in the day's meal just by how it tastes and looks. This is because our personality and intention come through in our food.

I think it's no exaggeration to say that other people can taste our mind and heart in our food. For example, some dishes are sloppily executed, but when you are eating them, you can tell whether this sloppiness is from ignorance and lack of experience or from willfulness. On the other hand, some cooks are quite good at technique but lack heart. Professional chefs become so good at technique that it masks their personality, which is why, if I'm traveling and eating in restaurants every day, I start to feel sad and empty. A home-cooked meal is nourishing because of the food itself, but also because it has been cooked with love and care.

The job of assistant to the abbess would rotate at the convent. When the time came for Chuho-san to be the abbess's assistant, I would sometimes be in the kitchen while she made bento for the abbess to take on a trip. Watching the compartments of delicate rice, vegetable, and egg components take shape as Chuho-san worked was always something of a wonder for me. How could someone make something so cute, delicious, and beautiful?

Now, though, I have no doubt that it was Chuho-san's love of her family that inspired her to become such a good cook — how else could she have woken up so early and worked for so long? I'm sure there were times when she resented the chore of making meals for her whole family while also holding down a full-time job. I'm sure she would have appreciated the extra hour of sleep or the downtime in the evening. But love is complicated like this. It is a mix of many feelings — affection and generosity but also obligation, resentment, and habit.

The summer I got married, I received a grant through my graduate program to travel to Japan for research on the history of Zen nuns. I had also — not coincidentally — planned to do the final ceremony in my Zen training, called *zuise*, which certified me to run a temple and have disciples, on the same trip. When I arrived in Japan, I found I was interested in neither Zen practice nor academic research. I dutifully completed that final *zuise* ceremony, showing up in the right outfit and bowing at the right times, and I followed up with all the leads I had for my research project, conducting interviews and securing obscure manuscripts and books. Yet all my thoughts were about food.

When my work was finished, I would spend hours in bookstores, buying up cheap bento recipe books (there are whole walls of bento cookbooks in used bookstores in Japan) or browsing the bento accessories at stationery and home-supply centers. I bought traditional bamboo boxes, small modern stacked lunch boxes, decorative toothpicks in the shape of panda bears, small plastic containers in the shape of green leaves, food molds, and instruction manuals. If it was about bento, I had to have it.

When I returned to the United States, I fell into the habit of making bento for Gensan three times a week. Modeling myself on the Japanese women I'd learned from, I planned the lunches over the weekend, mapping out which ingredients I would need when. I made detailed shopping lists. I julienned or sliced several cups of carrots, onions, and other vegetables, storing them in the refrigerator for easy use. I prepped the vegetables the night before and woke up at 6:30 to put on the final touches.

My favorite bento have a healthy portion of rice, something green, some kind of fried protein, and maybe another vegetable dish. Most bento have meat in them, but it's possible to imitate fried chicken or pork by using either tofu, *fu* (wheat gluten), or *koyadofu* (freeze-dried tofu).

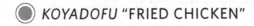 *KOYADOFU* "FRIED CHICKEN"

Serves 1

> 2 pieces (1 × 2 inches) *koyadofu* (freeze-dried tofu),
>   about 2 ounces
> 2 to 3 dried shiitake mushrooms soaked in
>   1 cup water for several hours
> 2 tablespoons soy sauce
> 1 tablespoon mirin
> 1 teaspoon sugar

1 teaspoon grated ginger (optional)
¼ cup cornstarch
1 tablespoon vegetable oil

Soak the *koyadofu* in water for 5 minutes until it is reconstituted and then cut it into bite-size pieces. Squeeze out the excess water.

Remove the shiitakes from the soaking liquid and to the liquid add the soy sauce, mirin, sugar, and ginger, if using. Soak the *koyadofu* in this mixture for several hours or overnight.

When you are ready to cook the *koyadofu*, remove it from the broth and gently squeeze out the excess liquid. Spread the cornstarch on a plate and dip the *koyadofu* in it until coated. Fry the *koyadofu* in the oil on medium about 3 minutes on each side, until golden brown.

Japanese women use special bento boxes, but it's not necessary to buy one. In the West, it's easy to find plastic reusable storage containers with built-in dividers, or you can use one large flat container. But if you want to use a Japanese bento box, by all means go ahead! They're easy enough to buy online or in a Japanese store. I think they're fun, so if you can get your hands on a Japanese bento box, you might as well use it.

To assemble the bento, if you are using a bento box, place the rice in the largest section, fill another section with the *koyadofu* "chicken," and in another place a green vegetable of your choice.

If you are using an undivided container, fill half of it with rice. Use a spatula or rice scooper to press the rice, so that it neatly fills up half of the container. Place a piece of green lettuce or beautiful sheet of paper at the edge of the rice to act as a divider. In the remaining space, carefully place the *koyadofu* "chicken" on one side and the green vegetable on the other. Make sure each ingredient is in its own space, separate from the others. To keep the food from mixing, you can use cupcake liners or more lettuce.

● GREEN BEANS IN SESAME SAUCE (*INGEN GOMAE*)

Gomae means "mixed with sesame." This sweet and luxurious method is an easy way to get a side dish that complements a spicy, vinegary, or oily main. The sesame seeds even make it high in protein (there are about 2 grams of protein in a tablespoon of sesame seeds). In place of green beans you can also substitute asparagus, broccoli, spinach, or whatever steamed vegetable you have on hand.

Serves 2 as a side dish

> 1 cup whole green beans
> 5 tablespoons ground sesame seeds
> 2 tablespoons mirin
> ½ teaspoon soy sauce
> ½ teaspoon dashi

Blanch the green beans whole in salted water for 2 minutes or until just tender. Drain and immediately cool them in a bowl of ice water. Once they are cool, cut them into 1-inch pieces.

Mix together the ground sesame seeds, mirin, soy sauce, and dashi. Add the green beans to the sesame sauce and mix gently to combine.

Once a month in Zen monasteries, monks and nuns undergo a period of intensive meditation known as *sesshin*, which lasts anywhere from three to seven days. The wake-up bell rings one hour earlier (3:00 instead of 4:00 AM!), the day's cleaning is completed in silence, and the whole day is spent in zazen. Meals are taken in silence, usually in the meditation hall, using the most formal form of *oryoki* practice.

At the monastery where I trained, the first day of *sesshin* we always had stewed soybeans, known in Japanese as *gomoku mame*, for breakfast. Whenever I eat these soybeans, I think of the breakfast on the first day of *sesshin* — that wonderful bite of hot, filling beans after a cold, silent morning.

FIVE-INGREDIENT SOYBEANS (*GOMOKU MAME*)

Gomoku mame has many variations, but they usually include soybeans, shiitakes, *konbu, konnyaku,* and carrots. In spite of the name, it can also have more than five ingredients and include such things as *abura age,* green beans, *hijiki* (edible seaweed), or whatever leftovers you have on hand.

This dish is by no means flashy. It doesn't use much extra dashi; most of the flavor comes from the water the soybeans are cooked in. *Gomoku mame* proves that simplicity, when done right, can be hearty and delicious.

Serves 4 as a side dish

> 1 cup dried soybeans soaked overnight in 2 cups water
> 1 cup water
> 1 to 2 teaspoons rice vinegar
> ½ cup diced (¼ inch) *renkon* (lotus root)
> 8 green beans
> 1 square (2 × 2 inches) *abura age* (fried tofu),
>   cut into ¼-inch strips
> 3 dried shiitake mushrooms soaked overnight in
>   enough water to cover

1 piece (4 × 4 inches) *konbu* (dried kelp) soaked in
      water to cover at least 4 hours or overnight
½ cup diced (¼ inch) carrot
¼ cup sake
3 tablespoons soy sauce
3 tablespoons mirin
2 teaspoons sugar
Salt to taste

After the soybeans have soaked, bring the beans and soaking liquid to a boil in a saucepan and cover with a lid. Cook on medium-low for 1 hour or more, until the soybeans are completely tender.

In a medium bowl combine the water and rice vinegar. While the soybeans cook, soak the *renkon* in the water and vinegar. Blanch the green beans in salted water for 2 minutes, rinse them with cold water, and slice them thinly on the diagonal. Pour some boiling water over the *abura age* and rinse it thoroughly with cold water to remove excess oil. Remove the shiitakes from the soaking liquid (reserve the liquid), squeeze them, and thinly slice them. Remove the *konbu* from its soaking liquid and cut it into ¼-inch pieces.

When the soybeans are tender, remove the *renkon* from its vinegar water and rinse it thoroughly. To the pot of soybeans, add the rinsed *renkon*, *abura age*, sliced mushrooms, *konbu*, carrots, sake, soy sauce, mirin, sugar, 2 tablespoons of the shiitake soaking liquid, and salt. Taste the broth and adjust the sugar and soy sauce to your liking. If it tastes too strongly of shiitake, add a little *konbu* powder to balance it out.

Simmer the vegetables on low for 15 minutes, until the carrots are tender and the *renkon* is no longer completely hard. When vegetables are done, turn off the heat and stir in the green beans. This dish can be served hot or chilled and makes a wonderful addition to a bento box.

The first time I sent Gensan to work with a bento, he took photos of the lunch and posted them on social media, and one of his coworkers snapped a photo of it and shared it on their group chat. He sent me screen shots of his coworkers comments. "Your fiancée is MAGIC AF," one of them exclaimed. I glowed with pride.

"Most of my coworkers have sad leftovers for lunch," he explained to me. In my head, I gave myself 1,000 invisible Fiancée Points, enough to put me leagues ahead of the other wives and girlfriends, I was sure.

I was proud of myself — proud of my effort and accomplishment, but also happy that I made him happy. I became more ambitious. Utilizing a rice mold in the shape of a cat, I made a bento with a landscape of cherry tomatoes, kale, and rice cats, complete with seaweed ears and eyes. When I closed my eyes to fall asleep at night, visions of bento boxes danced in my head. Lying awake, I would obsess about what to pair with leftover *kinpira* (a carrot stir-fry; see recipe on p. 169) or whether I had enough protein in the next day's box. All I could think about were bento.

But I was also writing and being a graduate student at the same time. I was testing recipes, making frequent trips to the grocery store, writing during the afternoon, and cooking dinner as well as attending class and doing coursework. Eventually I found I could not keep up with the elaborate boxed lunches and still do the other work I needed to do. Finally I admitted to Gensan that I was overwhelmed.

"Stop then," he encouraged me. "You have a book to write. Two books, if you count your master's thesis. I love the bento, but I can get lunch somewhere else. I don't want you to sacrifice your well-being for my happiness."

Slowly, the elaborate bento meals tapered off. Although I was happy to sleep in the extra hour, I missed them when they were gone.

Making bento is not difficult, but it is difficult to do every day. Recently, during a question-and-answer session after a book reading, an audience member asked me, "What do you think about the Japanese work ethic? Should we Americans be working harder?"

I paused, confused. It is not really my place to comment on the Japanese work ethic, since I am not Japanese. But I felt I could not ignore the question.

"Japanese culture produces some of the best food in the world," I said, "some of the most exquisite art. During the six years I lived in Japan, I only ever ate one bad meal in a restaurant. For the most part, every single meal you eat is one of the best meals of your life, because the work ethic is unrivaled and results in amazing products. But suicide and death from overwork are rampant in Japan. So I cannot say it is either good or bad."

The uncomfortable truth about women and cooking is that amazing meals are often a result of the strict societal demands on mothers and wives. Bento, as prepared by Japanese women, is truly an amazing and delicious thing. The effort women put into this is something to be grateful for, not critique. But those same societal demands compel mothers to be competitive with each other and cause women to want to prove their worth through their husbands and children, both of which have negative consequences. I believe the motivation women have for cooking is neither good nor bad — it produces both good and bad results.

I love to cook. I enjoy it. It is how I express love and care — as a woman, but also simply as a human. I enjoy cooking for my husband (there, I said it!), and if we ever have children, you better believe I will cook up a storm for them. It becomes a problem when I am taken for granted. In my mind, the problem is not gendered-biased views of cooking, but when those roles become expected, when the work is not reciprocal or balanced.

A year into our marriage, I am less concerned about what it means to be a wife. I just know I am one. Although I am a woman and he is a man, there is nothing gendered that defines me as a wife or him as a husband. Sex and gender are different. My sex is female, but my gender is not always female — it shifts depending on who I am dating and how I am feeling. We are husband and wife because we wanted commitment, not because we want to conform to gender roles. We have made our relationship about having a home, about making family, about loving each other, about radical honesty and vulnerability, about lifelong commitment.

Words have meaning, but often have a unique meaning for the person who speaks them. *Buddhism* means something unique to me, but it is probably different from what it means to you, even though when we both say the word, we approximate something similar. My *wife* to his *husband* is uniquely mine, because our marriage is uniquely ours.

In the summer of 2018, after I'd finished my graduate program, we moved to San Francisco, so that I could be closer to my family as well as attend (another) graduate program to train to become a therapist. Gensan started a new job the second weekend after we moved. I was standing in the kitchen, slicing carrots for a fried rice, when I realized his first day of work was approaching. I really wanted to make him a bento to take that day. We had spent the last few days unpacking and looking for new furniture. That week I had been stressed and haggard from sleeping on an air mattress, and he had been overwhelmed by the move. We had been arguing almost non-stop about typical, domestic problems like what color the new couch should be and where the bookcases should go.

"Can I make you bento tomorrow?" I asked, once again grasping for food to remedy an unstable set of circumstances.

I imagined spending hours in the kitchen slicing vegetables into tiny pieces, pressing rice into molds to create whimsical food landscapes. I remembered the colors of tomatoes and cartoon-decorated wrappers, the satisfaction I felt closing the lid on a beautiful box of food that I knew would make him happy. I remembered feeling proud of my effort, and exhausted, all before 7:30 AM. I remembered feeling secure and in control.

"It's okay," he told me. "We have catered lunch at this job."

I was disappointed. It would have been so nice and easy to send him to work with a bento, to feel confident in a role as a wife who takes care of her husband with food. Like being a nun, like being a saint, how simple and exhausting being a good woman is! But that was not who we were, not really. It was San Francisco in the twenty-first century, I was busy, and he worked at a company that served catered lunches.

I went back to cooking dinner, but when I closed my eyes that night, I saw tiny plastic containers in the shapes of leaves.

Christmas is arguably the biggest holiday for the majority of North Americans — signifying family, presents, and food — whereas in Japan Christmas is almost humorously known as a "lovers' holiday," much like Valentine's Day. Japanese Christmas is when young couples adjourn to "love hotels," kitschy themed rooms that you can rent by the hour for all of your amorous needs.

On the other hand, in Japan New Year's is the winter holiday akin to Christmas, when people travel across the country to be with their families for days of celebration, ceremony, and food. For many Japanese, New Year's is synonymous with *osechi ryori*, or New Year's food, served in a multiple-tiered lacquer box. This special New Year's box is filled with a variety of special food that the family (usually the mother) spends literally weeks preparing beforehand. Some traditional New Year's foods are fish cakes, kelp rolls stuffed with salmon, *chikuzenni* (see Simmered Root Vegetables, p. 157), and of course *namasu*, sliced carrot and daikon in a sweet vinegary sauce.

At Nisodo we would break off into small groups or pairs to prepare New Year's food, with each group assigned one kind of delicacy. The first year I was there, when I still didn't know how to cook well, *namasu* was the one dish they trusted me to help make. I paired up with an older nun and dutifully sliced buckets and buckets of daikon and carrots into tiny strips, while she was in charge of making the vinegar marinade.

On New Year's Eve we stayed up well past midnight performing special chants and helping the local parishioners ring the giant temple bell 108 times for good luck. In the morning we rose at 5:00, did our usual cleaning and chanting, and then ate a breakfast of *osechi ryori* and sake. The only time I ever saw alcohol in the temple was on New Year's. I will never forget the sensation of being sleep-deprived, eating seaweed rolls stuffed with fish for breakfast (and trying not to gag in the process), and getting drunk on sake at 7:00 in the morning! A very "Zen" experience, if you ask me.

⦿ JULIENNED DAIKON AND CARROT
IN SWEET VINEGAR SAUCE (*NAMASU*)

Namasu is a traditional New Year's dish, but it works well any time of the year or in bento. Because it's sweet and vinegary, you probably don't want to eat more than half a cup of this, but it makes the perfect counterpoint to heavier fried or stewed food.

Serves 2 as a side dish

> 1 piece (2½ inches) daikon
> 1 piece (1½ inches) carrot
> 2 teaspoons salt
> 1 tablespoon rice vinegar
> 1 tablespoon sugar
> ½ teaspoon soy sauce
> ½ teaspoon finely sliced yuzu (Japanese lemon) peel
>   or yuzu zest (optional)

Using a mandolin or carrot peeler, slice the daikon into thin strips. Then, using a sharp knife, cut the strips into long, thin slices. They should be about 2 inches long and as thin as possible. Repeat with the carrot, and then place both together in a mixing bowl.

Sprinkle the salt over the vegetable mixture. Using your hands, massage the salt into the daikon and carrots. Let them sit until water starts to collect in the bottom of the bowl, about 30 minutes. Using a cloth or paper towel, squeeze out the excess water and place the vegetables in a dry plastic container.

In a bowl, mix together the vinegar, sugar, and soy sauce until the sugar is dissolved. Pour this over the daikon and carrot strips, and stir to mix. Add the yuzu peel or zest, stir, and then refrigerate overnight. This dish will keep in the refrigerator for several weeks.

SIMMERED ROOT VEGETABLES (*CHIKUZENNI*)

Another New Year's food, *chikuzenni* is actually a delicacy that in its most rarified form is served in a tiered lacquer box, with the carrots and lotus root shaped like flowers, the shiitakes engraved with an immaculate star design, and floral garnishes. New Year's food is designed to be eaten for several days in a row, so you can see how this would make the easy transition into a bento box. It can be a humble, simple stew or a fancy one and even crops up in supermarkets and delis.

I remember reading this recipe in a book when I was working in the kitchen at Nisodo, probably when I was in charge of creating the menus. The recipe called for chicken, but we of course didn't have that, so I just omitted it. In my mind, *chikuzenni* feels like a classic homemaker dish; you can tell it was invented by throwing all of the fall vegetables on hand into one pot and then cooking them together.

Serves 3 to 4 as a side dish

> 2 dried shiitake mushrooms soaked in water to cover
>   for at least 4 hours
> 1 cup thinly sliced *gobo* (burdock root)
> 1 cup bite-size diagonally cut *renkon* (lotus-root) pieces
> 2 cups water
> 3 tablespoons rice vinegar
> 15 snow pea pods
> 2 teaspoons vegetable oil
> 1 cup bite-size diagonally cut carrot pieces
> 2 tablespoons thinly sliced ginger
> 2 cups dashi (or use the shiitake soaking liquid)
> 3 tablespoons sake
> 3 tablespoons mirin
> 1 teaspoon sugar
> 3 tablespoons soy sauce

Remove the shiitakes from the soaking liquid and reserve it for cooking, either in this dish or in another. Cut the mushrooms into quarters. Soak the *gobo* in water for at least 30 minutes. Soak the *renkon* for 30 minutes in the 2 cups water and vinegar. Drain and rinse all the vegetables.

Blanch the snow peas in salted water for 90 seconds. Drain and immediately plunge them into a bowl of ice water. When cool, remove them from the water and cut them in half on the diagonal.

Heat the oil in a pan and add the shiitakes, *gobo*, *renkon*, and carrots. Sauté the vegetables on high for 2 minutes, until they begin to change color. Add the ginger and sauté for another minute. Next, add the dashi and cook on medium-low for 10 minutes, or until the dashi has reduced by half. After the dashi has reduced, add the sake, mirin, sugar, and soy sauce. Put a small lid or piece of foil on top of the vegetables to keep them submerged under the broth and continue to cook for another 10 minutes until vegetables are tender and the broth is almost completely reduced.

Just before serving, mix in the blanched snow peas.

Meal Ideas: Serve warm with rice; Miso Soup (p. 54) with tofu and wakame; and a vinegar dish such as Julienned Daikon and Carrot in Sweet Vinegar Sauce (p. 156). Or serve cold in a bento box.

● TOFU-STUFFED PEPPERS

Okara (tofu pulp) is a delicious and versatile meat substitute. In the monastery kitchen where I worked, we would often use leftover *okara* dishes (such as Sautéed Vegetables and Tofu Pulp, p. 22) to make vegan hamburgers, croquettes, or stuffing for *piman*, Japanese green peppers. Stewed *okara* is admittedly a little runny, so if you'd rather stuff your peppers with something a little more substantial than leftovers (or if you've eaten them already), you can create fresh stuffing with *okara*, tofu, oats, and vegetables. I've eaten variations on this dish many times at the monastery, although we never had oats on hand. I think the oats add a nice extra crunch, but you could also use cooked rice if you'd like to stay with strictly traditional Japanese ingredients.

Serves 4

    2 cups *okara* (tofu pulp)
    4 *piman* (Japanese green peppers)
    3 tablespoons vegetable oil, *divided*
    ½ cup minced yellow onion
    ½ cup minced carrot
    1 tablespoon minced ginger
    Salt and pepper
    1 cup silken tofu, blended
    ½ cup instant oats or cooked rice
    Cornstarch or potato starch
    ¼ cup *panko* (Japanese bread crumbs)
    Ponzu sauce or ketchup, for serving

Before using *okara*, make sure it has been dry-fried until it resembles hot sand. Place the *okara* in a bowl.

Cut the *piman* in half lengthwise and remove the stem and white membrane. Place the *piman* halves in a bowl of water and use your hands to remove the seeds. Dry the *piman* and set aside.

Heat 1 tablespoon of the oil in a frying pan and sauté the onion and carrot on low until the onions begin to change color, about 3 minutes. Add the ginger and continue sautéing until onions are translucent. Season with salt and pepper.

Add the cooked vegetables, blended tofu, and oats to the

okara. Gently stir until combined. Season generously with salt. Coat the insides of the *piman* with cornstarch and then dip them in cornstarch so that the outsides are coated as well. With your hands, scoop up the *okara* mixture and fill the pepper halves with it, about 2 to 3 tablespoons per pepper, depending on their size. Firmly press the *okara* into the pepper halves, so it stays in place. Sprinkle *panko* over the top of the stuffed peppers.

Fry the peppers in 2 tablespoons of oil on medium, covered. Fry for 3 minutes with the pepper side down; then flip and cook until the tops are golden brown. Serve with ponzu sauce or ketchup.

Meal Idea: Serve with rice; Miso Soup (p. 54) with pumpkin, shimeji mushrooms, and green onions; and Green Beans in Sesame Sauce (p. 148), if using ponzu, or Crushed Cucumber and Tomato Salad (p. 26), if using ketchup.

WINTER FESTIVAL CANDIED YAMS (*DAIGAKU IMO*)

If these caramelized yams seem more like dessert to you than a sensible side dish, then you're probably right. But step outside into the streets on a cold winter day in Japan, and you're bound to encounter these delicious sweet bites somewhere. They're popular snacks at local festivals or piping hot from a food truck that has been driving slowly through town, blaring a recording of a song about yams. Japanese yams (*satsumaimo*) have purple skin and yellow flesh, but if you can't find the Japanese kind, you can use sweet potatoes or even regular potatoes. During the winter at the monastery, when potatoes were plentiful and green vegetables were scarce, we would make this dish to add variety to the normal potato-dish rotation.

Sometimes the nuns would even mix yams and potatoes together if there weren't enough yams.

I remember approaching Chuho-san, the cook at Nisodo,
the first time I ate these. I exclaimed how wonderful they were,
and she sort of shrugged. "They're just children's snacks," she
responded. "And we don't have any actual vegetables in the
cellar."

There are several ways to prepare *daigaku imo*, but this is
the way I like.

Serves 2 as a side dish

> 1½ cups bite-size pieces (or sticks) *satsumaimo*
> (Japanese yams), sweet potatoes, or potatoes
> ¼ cup vegetable oil
> 3 tablespoons sugar
> 1 teaspoon soy sauce
> 1 tablespoon water
> ½ teaspoon salt
> 1 teaspoon black sesame seeds, for garnish

Soak the yams in water for 15 minutes. Drain and pat dry.

Heat the oil in a large frying pan. Add the cut yams so
that they are in a single layer and fry them without stirring for
1½ minutes. Flip the yams and continue frying, stirring frequently, until they are tender and all sides are golden brown,
about 10 minutes. Remove the yams from the oil and place
them on paper towels to absorb excess oil.

Mix together the sugar, soy sauce, water, and salt. Add
the sauce mixture to a clean frying pan and heat until it bub-
bles, about 30 seconds. Add the yams and stir them into
the sauce, cooking on medium for another 2 minutes, until
the yams are coated and the sauce has caramelized. Carefully

watch the sauce during this step, since it can burn if the heat is too high.

Serve hot, garnished with black sesame seeds.

The word *karma* means "action" in Sanskrit, but the concept has entered the popular lexicon as shorthand for "revenge" or "cosmic comeuppance," as when people say, "Karma is a bitch," or Taylor Swift in "Look What You Made Me Do" sings that karma is the only thing she thinks about and reminds her enemies that "they'll get theirs" (in other words, they will be punished for hurting her).

But karma is not punitive. It is not about right or wrong. I like to think about karma as the totality of our lived experience (that is, our actions and the actions of those around us). The best way to understand karma is to look at where you are in the present moment. What brought you to this place, to this feeling, to this way of being? Karma is our actions and simultaneously the consequences of those actions.

I don't believe in the kind of karma written about in traditional Buddhist texts, where all problems, from zits to poverty to congenital abnormalities, are attributed to our past lives. That is a cruel way to view social inequality. But sometimes events occur that are so clearly the result of past action that I can't help but attribute them to karma.

For example, when I was in a bento frenzy, I bought a bunch of fancy bento boxes for my husband, as I mentioned earlier in the chapter. I never would have bought such elaborate containers for myself. When we moved to San Francisco, he started a job that provided a catered lunch, and I found myself strapped for cash due to graduate-school payments. One evening I decided to make my lunch for tomorrow instead of buying it. I would make my ideal bento. The bento combination I came up with was rice, a package of natto (fermented soybeans), and the dish below, which is everything I want — protein, vegetables, and a little bit of sweetness. It was a delicious treat for myself, made all the more satisfying by realizing it resulted from my past actions.

● KARMIC TOFU AND VEGGIES

Makes 1 bento serving

> 1 bunch *komatsuna* or spinach
> ½ carrot, cut into bite-size chunks
> 1½ cups dashi
> 2 tablespoons sake
> 1 tablespoon sugar
> 1½ tablespoons soy sauce
> 4 ounces thick roasted tofu cubes with brown edges
>   (such as *atsu age* or Organic Tofu Cutlet from
>   House Foods)
> ¼ bunch shimeji mushrooms (about 1 ounce)

Blanch the *komatsuna* whole in salted water for 1 to 2 minutes and then drain it. Let it cool down a bit so that you can touch it with your hands and wring out the excess water. Cut it into 1-inch pieces.

In a small saucepan bring the carrots and dashi to a boil. Cook for 4 minutes on high. Stir in the sake and sugar; then lower the heat and cook for 3 to 5 minutes, or until the carrots are tender. Add the soy sauce, tofu, and mushrooms and continue cooking on medium-low for 10 to 20 minutes, or until the tofu has darkened by absorbing the soy sauce. Salt to taste and then gently stir in the blanched *komatsuna*.

11

END MEANS BEGINNING

Leftovers

W hile I was living at Nisodo, I was given the opportunity to do my head monk's ceremony, called *hossenshiki* in Japanese. This is a coming-of-age ritual in which a novice priest moves closer toward full certification. It takes a lot of preparation, practice, and hard work to learn the complicated service, especially memorizing the predetermined sequence of bowing that must be followed. The *hossenshiki* lasts over an hour and is followed by Dharma combat in which the *shusso*, or "head monk" (in this case, me), engages in a scripted, highly dramatic (screaming!) debate with his or her peers on classical Japanese Zen doctrine and the true meaning of practice.

The day of my *hossenshiki*, I dressed in a brand-new silk robe I had been given for the occasion. I put on *besu*, the formal white socks used by Zen clergy in Japan, and gathered with the other nuns in the waiting room. My teacher and friends from the monastery where I had been ordained had come to visit and were seated in the Buddha hall. A complicated sequence of drums, bells, and clackers signaled the beginning of the event. As the drumroll swelled, I marched in procession with the other nuns and entered the hall, my heart pounding. What if I froze? What if I forgot my lines?

When the cue came for me to speak, I gripped a black bamboo staff in my hands, took a deep breath, and yelled the opening line as loud as I could in the fierce, bellowing style I had been taught.

"Listen!" I yelled in classical Japanese, a style of speaking closer to medieval poetry than contemporary conversation. "This staff is a three-foot long snake. On Vulture Peak it became the *udumbara* flower....Now, in accord with the order of my teacher, it lies in my hands!"

The words tumbled out of me, in Japanese and then in English, without my even having to think about them. The more I yelled, the less nervous I felt.

There is a point in the ceremony when the head monk apologizes for his or her failures. Within the context of Japanese culture, this demonstrates neither remorse nor shame, but humility and a healthy sense of connection to the community. When the time came for me to apologize, I was overcome with both gratitude and a sense of my relative smallness compared to the rest of the global Buddhist community, and tears streamed down my face.

After the *hossenshiki*, relief washed over me. As I thanked the people at the monastery for their assistance, I encountered Eko-san, an older, wise nun who often helped me in the kitchen, explained the more difficult parts of monastic procedures, or gave me advice when I was arguing with another nun. Eko-san is one of the most practical, hands-on people I have ever met. Although she is the abbess of a small Zen temple in Nagoya, her teaching does not devolve into inscrutable Zen riddles; she prefers instead to point out a more straightforward way of doing or thinking.

"I'm finished!" I said to her happily.

She smiled and then responded in Japanese, "End means beginning."

In Japan they say, "A monk's mouth is like an oven." I was told this over and over again at Nisodo when the *tenzo* served up something that didn't taste good. Older nuns scolded strict vegetarians visiting the monastery with this proverb too, because sometimes temple members donated meat. Since monks and nuns traditionally beg for a living, we were supposed to cultivate a nonjudgmental attitude about food. Beyond the literal interpretation, this proverb also means that we should not be picky about external situations in our life. We should ingest them all as they come — difficult, loud, painful, pleasant, or humorous — and use them for fuel. We do not always have the privilege of choosing what our spiritual path will be — it is always eating the "food" that life serves us.

If learning to eat at the monastery was acclimating to the practice of consuming whatever was put in from of me, learning to cook at the monastery was a lesson in how to take care of ingredients. Dogen Zenji wrote, "Not to waste a single grain of rice is called the mind of the way." This has a similar but slightly different meaning from "A monk's mouth is like an oven." The emphasis is on the cook rather than the eater. What Dogen is saying is that not wasting food — taking care of the material around you and preserving what you have — is the totality of Zen life. Zen is difficult, but it is not complicated. It is simply taking care of things.

At the monasteries where I trained, there was an explicit admonition to never throw away food. At Nisodo, meals were calculated down to the precise half bowl of soup, and any left-overs were eaten at dinnertime, mixed into soup or savory rice porridge. We first figured out how many people were expected at the meal. With soup, for example, each person was allotted a bowl and a half; this assured that everyone had at least one serving and then that those who wanted seconds could have them. This is actually very basic common sense. It just involves foresight — for example, knowing how big the bowls are, how much food fits into one bowl, and how much vegetables shrink during cooking.

The Japanese phrase *mottainai* is used to express displeasure about wasting. It can be translated as "Don't waste!" and it's used to describe instances of throwing away either tangible or intangible things. For example, when I told a young woman in Japan that I didn't want to get married, she exclaimed, "You're young! *Mottainai!*" Back in the United States, when I lament my declining Japanese skills, people often agree, "*Mottainai!*" And of course, in Japan, if the nuns and I ever considered throwing away some week-old tub of leftover soup, someone would inevitably utter "*Mottainai!*" And the soup would end up as part of our dinner or creatively incorporated into another dish.

Conserving and respecting food involves equal parts planning how much to cook and repurposing leftovers and old produce. I am not quite sure why I never questioned the reason for peeling carrots until I worked in a monastery kitchen. But really, what is the point of peeling carrots? *Mottainai!* They taste the same with or without the peel, and the peel contains extra nutrients.

If you must peel your carrots, scrub them thoroughly and save the peels. Add them to soup or make *kinpira*, the sweet and spicy Japanese stir-fry that traditionally uses carrots and *gobo*.

◉ SAUTÉED CARROT PEEL (*KINPIRA*)

To shave the *gobo*, "sharpen" the root to a point like a pencil and then shave off thin strips, turning the root in your hand between slices to keep the shavings an equal size.

Serves 2 to 3 as a side dish

> 2 cups thinly julienned or shaved *gobo* (burdock root)
> 2 teaspoons vegetable oil
> 1 cup carrot peels
> 2½ tablespoons soy sauce
> 2½ tablespoons mirin
> 1 tablespoon sake
> Drizzle of sesame oil
> Sesame seeds, for garnish (optional)

Soak the *gobo* in water for at least 30 minutes. This softens it and makes it easier to cook as well as removing some of the bitterness. Drain the *gobo*.

Heat the vegetable oil in a wide frying pan and add the *gobo*. Sauté the *gobo* until soft, about 4 minutes (test a sliver of *gobo* to make sure; it should be soft with the tiniest bit of resistance in your mouth, but not at all crunchy).

Add the carrot peel and cook for 30 seconds. Add the soy sauce, mirin, and sake and continue to cook, stirring frequently, until the vegetables are coated. Turn off the heat and add a drizzle of sesame oil (a little bit goes a long way) and sesame seeds.

Variation: You can also substitute leftover daikon peel for the *gobo* (for example, from making Daikon "Steak," on p. 41). Daikon peels and carrot peels soften in roughly the same amount of time, so you will want to add them to the pan together. Then cook and season as above.

◉ FRIED POTATO PEELS

The monks at Eiheiji, one of the two main Soto Zen monasteries, have nifty ways of reinvigorating just about any vegetable scrap — even potato peelings. Deep-fried, liberally sprinkled with salt, and eaten while hot, they taste just like organic potato chips — which they are!

Servings vary

Potato peels from thoroughly scrubbed potatoes
Vegetable oil for deep-frying
Salt

In a bowl soak the peels in enough water to cover for at least 2 hours. Drain and dry them completely between two cloths or paper towels.

Pour at least 1½ inches of oil into a large deep pan and heat to between 350 and 370°F. (Or if you have a deep-fryer, use it following the manufacturer's directions.) When the oil is hot, deep-fry the peels. They will cook very quickly, in under a minute. Remove them from the oil and place on paper towels to absorb excess oil. Salt them generously and serve immediately.

◉ FRIED NOODLES (*YAKI UDON*)

Day-old noodles are fun to cook with and can be even more satisfying than the original dish. At the monastery I always hoped there would be leftover udon, so that we could eat *yaki udon* the next day. *Yaki udon* are fried noodles that are more akin to bar food than high cuisine. Before I became acclimated to Japanese tastes, *yaki udon* was the first dish at the monastery I truly loved, because it is greasy, sloppy, inelegant, and satisfying — in other words, it's more akin to American food than traditional monastery fare. It can also be made with spaghetti instead of udon.

Yakiniku sauce, also known as *tonkatsu* sauce or Japanese barbecue sauce, is easily found in any Asian or well-stocked American grocery store.

Serves 2

> ½ onion, sliced
> 1 carrot, cut into ¼-inch-wide strips
> 1 tablespoon vegetable oil
> ¼ cabbage, cut into bite-size pieces
> 1 bunch shimeji mushrooms, separated, or ½ cup
>   of another mushroom, thinly sliced
> 10½ ounces leftover plain udon or spaghetti
>   (about 3½ cups)
> ¼ cup *yakiniku* sauce, or to taste
> Salt and pepper to taste
> Ketchup to taste

In a large pan or wok, sauté the onion and carrot in the vegetable oil on medium-high until softened. Add the cabbage and cook another 2 minutes, until the cabbage begins to soften. Add the shimeji mushrooms and give the whole pan a hearty stir. (If you are using a different kind of mushroom that takes longer to cook, add it earlier, with the onion and carrot.) Salt the vegetables.

Push the vegetables to the side of the pan. Separate the noodles and add them to the open space in the pan. Sauté the noodles, stirring constantly, for 30 seconds and then stir to incorporate the vegetables into the noodles. When noodles are heated through and vegetables are soft but not mushy, add the *yakiniku* sauce and mix until everything is coated in a thin layer.

Turn off the heat and taste. Add more sauce, salt, pepper, or ketchup as needed.

⬤ GOLDEN CURRY

Golden Curry is a meal so easy to whip up it does not really warrant its own recipe. It's one of the few meals I trust my husband to prepare without looking over his shoulder the whole time, offering neurotic suggestions. It's a not-so-spicy Japanese take on Indian curry, most commonly made by using packets of roux that dissolves easily in hot water and thickens into a curry sauce. I mention it here because curry is one of the best ways to get rid of leftovers. Anything can go into curry — old noodles, vegetables, and even lettuce. It's best not to add anything that already has a distinctive flavor, such as potato salad or vinegar-flavored dishes. But leftover Meat 'n' Potatoes for Zen Monks (p. 24) and other stewed vegetable dishes blend seamlessly with curry.

Serves 3

> 1 tablespoon vegetable oil
> ½ large onion, diced medium
> 2 carrots, cut into bite-size pieces
> 2 large potatoes, peeled and cut into bite-size pieces
> 1 cup leftovers you feel bad about wasting, such as
>   plain tofu, tomatoes, green beans, lettuce, etc.
> 4 squares (1 × 1 inch each) curry roux

Heat the oil in a deep frying pan, pot, or wok and add the onions. Stir-fry on medium for 2 minutes, until the onions begin to soften. Add the carrots and potatoes and continue to stir-fry for another 3 to 5 minutes, until the vegetables are beginning to soften but have not yet browned.

Add water to the pan until it is 1 inch above the vegetables.

Bring to a boil and cook until the potatoes are completely soft, another 10 to 15 minutes. If your leftovers are raw, add them so they get their requisite cooking time and are done when the potatoes are fully cooked. For example, if you are adding green beans, add them about 2 minutes before the potatoes will be done. If your leftovers are already cooked, you can add them at the very end.

Add the roux squares to the boiling water in the pan. Stir, breaking up the roux, until it is completely dissolved (you can also dice or slice the roux before adding it to make sure it doesn't clump). Continue stirring until the sauce thickens. The consistency should be like yogurt — thick enough that it is clearly not liquid, but soft and gelatinous. If the curry sauce isn't thickening, add more roux, one piece at a time, waiting a minute between each piece and stirring constantly, until it reaches the desired consistency.

It is fairly easy to preserve food and deal with leftovers in a Zen monastery, where there is an explicit value placed on not wasting. It is harder to do in a contemporary American household, which is not set up the same way. When I first moved in with Gensan, I tried to save as much as I could. I kept every last scrap of leftovers in the refrigerator and refused to throw away vegetables until they were rotten. If vegetables did go bad before I had a chance to cook them, I mourned their loss. I put old vegetables in soup. I conserved.

But after six months of comfortable domesticity, I found that the refrigerator was packed full of rotting leftovers, half-eaten or rarely used sauce, and obscure oil that I bought on a whim. I had slipped right back into the American way of grocery shopping when I was anxious, stressed, or upset. I stocked the pantry to feel I had a handle on my life, that I was competent as an adult, that I was taking care of my family. I only used a fraction of what I bought.

If you notice you have fallen into this habit, make a list of everything in your refrigerator. That's right — get an actual piece of paper and write down each and every vegetable, plastic container, and sauce. It's helpful to divide things into sections like leftovers, produce, and so on. For example, the current contents of my refrigerator are:

- **Leftovers:** takeout rice and vegetables with peanut sauce from a Thai restaurant
- **Old produce:** green onions, cilantro, cucumbers, baby bok choi, avocados (very brown), carrots, onions, garlic, limes, cherry tomatoes
- **Other:** salsa, mustard, peanut butter, sambal oelek, ketchup, tomato sauce, Sriracha, miso, tahini, soy sauce

When you look at these items as a list rather than as amorphous unwanted refrigerator contents, it becomes easy to figure out ways to use them. Stare at your list for a bit and allow the ingredients to dance in front of you; then look for natural resonances between foods and flavor profiles. For example, in the above list avocados and cherry tomatoes with some minced onion, garlic, and lime juice would make a nice guacamole-salsa dip (and I do have chips!). The tiny amount of leftover Thai food could be revamped with the addition of stir-fried onion, bok choi, and carrots in a spicy peanut sauce. If I combined peanut butter, soy sauce, chili oil, sesame oil, and sugar, I would get a delicious sauce (with a kick) that I could garnish with the aging cilantro and green onions.

This is a chance to be creative, to utilize and make the most of the material at hand. Then when you go grocery shopping the next time, write down what you put into the refrigerator and on what date. Cross out food that gets eaten or discarded, so you always know what you have. Using this method, you can keep your refrigerator a lot more civil, and you can train yourself to take care of produce and old food.

Eat what is put in front of you and take care of leftovers. Consume the circumstances of your life, whatever they are, and turn them into fuel. Take care of your community, your house, your family, and your pantry.

On a Monday morning in my second year at USC, I woke up at 7:30. I instinctually reached for my phone (nasty habit) and saw a bunch of new work emails. I groaned, turned off my phone, and closed my eyes again. My husband was still sleeping. I could hear the dog crying in the kennel next to our bed, where she sleeps; she likes the kennel, but by morning she's lonely. When my alarm went off ten minutes later, my husband put his arms around me. "I love you," he murmured sleepily. "And the dog loves you. She knows you're awake, and she wants to see you."

We lay entangled in each other for a few more minutes. "Mondays are evil," he groaned. I agreed. We tore ourselves from the bed and got ready — he for his job, and me for the Downtown Women's Center, where I volunteered.

I had been inspired to give my time to the shelter after working during the summer in Los Angeles at a drug and alcohol rehabilitation clinic founded by a famous Buddhist teacher. It was my first time working in a mental-health setting, and I loved it — it was the first time in my life I knew what I wanted to do. My routine was to breathalyze the clients twice a day, take their blood pressure while they were detoxing, and give out the assigned medicine, but most of the time my job was simply to be the responsible authority figure people could talk to. I made smoothies in the communal kitchen and listened to clients' stories while I cooked. Sometimes their stories were of heartbreak and trauma, but they also talked about their families, children, dogs, and opinions on music and tattoos.

During that period of working at a rehab, I realized I could do this for a living if I wanted to. I could get paid to be kind and calm and listen to people. Eventually, I applied to graduate programs in counseling psychology, so that I could begin the process of becoming a therapist. When my academic school year started up again, I signed up to volunteer at the Downtown Women's Center, a resource center for homeless women, so I could get more experience interacting with the addicted and mentally ill. I was still studying Japanese history and Buddhism at USC, but I could feel my heart turning toward something else.

After a slow start that morning, I finally got all my things together, put my schoolbooks and laptop in my backpack along with my lunch and headed out the door. The bus let me off at 6th Street and Broadway in downtown Los Angeles. I headed east down 6th toward San Pedro Street, an area of Los Angeles called "Skid Row" (this is an actual neighborhood in the city, populated by around six thousand homeless people). I immediately regretted not riding the bus one stop farther. For whatever reason, approaching the women's center from the north isn't so bad, but I'm afraid every time I walk down 6th Street.

I wonder if there will come a time when I will not be scared walking through Skid Row. Sometimes I brag that I am not afraid of people. "I've traveled alone in India," I say. "I'm not afraid of poverty." It's true. I have traveled alone in India, but this is different. In the slums of India there is extreme poverty, but there are families, mothers, and children. There are no families in this neighborhood. There are very few women, even.

As I walked down the sidewalk, I could smell urine and feel my heartbeat quicken. On either side of the road were tents and people sleeping on the ground. Across the street, a man and a woman were in a screaming argument that looked as if it was going to turn violent. I wondered if they were lovers or if he was her pimp. I sped up my pace, wondering if it was stupid of me to pack my laptop in my backpack. Finally I turned the corner onto San Pedro.

An odd thing about Skid Row is that the farther you walk into it, the less the laws and city institutions seem to apply. No one obeys traffic lights. There are very few cars. There are no businesses other than shelters. It's like a war zone or scene in a movie after the apocalypse. People spill out onto the sidewalks, sleep on cardboard or curled up against the walls, or stand side by side, smoking. Their bodies are thin, faces haggard from lack of sleep, food, medicine, and affection from other human beings.

When I reached the women's center, I relaxed. Men are not allowed there except for employees, most of whom are women. The homeless women sit in the day center — a large room with tables and chairs — and do drawing activities, learn to type, get health checkups, or eat lunch. That Monday I was assigned to sort donated clothes into piles of shirts, pants, tank tops, shoes, and sweaters for an event called "Shopping," where women can choose five of their favorite clothing items from the piles. Someone had donated a whole bag of unused bathing suits. There was a surprising amount of body-con clothing — formfitting dresses, leotards, and lingerie. My job was to sit next to the clothes and check to see that women only took five items. One woman chose only scarves. One woman seemed keen on lingerie. Another stuffed far more than five items into a purse.

The women who come to the center lack hygiene products, shoes, food, money, clothes, homes, and often families. They can be survivors of domestic violence who turn to drugs to help ease the pain and trauma they have experienced or their feelings of helplessness and anger. Or they are women who simply cannot afford the rent in the largely gentrifying neighborhoods of Los Angeles. Or they are suffering from mental illness. Or they are immigrants. Or they are all of these things.

After "Shopping" was over, I covered a table in the middle of the day center with a black plastic bag and then lugged over a giant box filled with dozens of bottles of nail polish. For the next hour I sat at the table and talked to the women who came by to paint their nails. Some of them were looking forward to birthday parties or job interviews. "I wanna look professional," several told me. One woman seemed more tenuously connected to reality, placing her bare feet on the table (despite my repeated insistence that we were not allowed to paint toes) and slathering on green polish until her heels were streaked with green.

I didn't say very much while staffing the nail station, preferring to listen. One woman talked continuously about Jesus. Another, I realized, had been swearing at me under her breath for the past ten minutes.

I glanced in her direction, wondering for a second if I had done something wrong — perhaps I had excluded her or had spilled polish on her.

"You're fucking bullshit," she snarled at me. "You're disgusting."

Not for the first time that day, I felt my chest lurch in fear. My body clenched, and my heart beat faster. I looked around, locating the security guard who always stood at the door. But the woman's words were just words. Eventually she stood up and walked away from the table, sputtering expletives. I continued painting my nails and chatting with the other women about their color choices.

Twenty minutes later she approached me to apologize. "I'm sorry I was rude," she said. "That wasn't okay."

"It's all right," I said, relieved.

American culture is not set up in a manner that values preservation. In fact, the message our culture sends us says the opposite — that we should always purchase the new thing, the coolest or freshest thing. We are told that if our refrigerator and pantry are not completely stocked to the brim, we are not successful, we are not providing for our family. The problem with this is not accumulation in and of itself, but that we are not taught how to take care of and value the things we already have.

The same is true with people. People are only worthy of our time and attention if they have value to us personally, if they conform to social norms, if they are easy, pleasant, and attractive. We divide people into categories like "successful," "failures," "contributors," "leeches," "motivated," "useless," "lazy." Then we allow these words to become the totality of a human being.

We are afraid of difference and weakness. We are afraid of poor people because of the labels we create, and then we become ashamed of our hate and fear. Instead of examining our shame and fear, we keep society's outcasts at a distance. We treat them like trash and throw them away. We make laws saying they cannot sleep in tents. We make laws saying they cannot sleep on benches. We say they did this to themselves, that they "chose" this life, when nothing could be farther from the truth. (No woman wants to sleep on concrete; it is very painful, not to mention unsafe.) We say they are someone else's problem. We forget they are human beings just like us.

Bernie Glassman, the Zen teacher famous for his work with the homeless, explained that when we care for the outcasts in society, we are caring for the parts of ourselves that we have rejected, the parts of ourselves we hate or feel shame about. It took me many months before I realized that this is what I was trying to do in my work with addicted clients. Working with people who relapsed over and over, I saw how easily I was frustrated by my clients, how quickly I moved to judgment and then to an impulse to discard them, to punish them by withdrawing kindness and compassion.

Abbess Aoyama Roshi would often say, "How you spend your time is how you live your life." Spiritual practice shows us that the way we relate to small things — washing dishes, cooking, waiting, cleaning — is indicative of how we relate to everything else. The training in Zen practice is learning how to take care of even the smallest, most mundane task, because the task in front of you is the totality of the universe. So eventually I began to see that the way I was relating to addicted people was how I related to myself. I saw that when I was tired, sad, or struggling, when I didn't receive labels like "successful," "beautiful," "rich," and "competent," I hated myself. I felt like trash.

I want to have compassion for the parts of myself I hate — my anger and selfishness, my lust, my introversion, my seriousness. I want to have compassion for these because they are everything that makes me *me*. But it is hard. We are taught to hate difficult things, difficult emotions, anything that does not contribute to a well-functioning individual. Part of me knows that, in order to have compassion for the world around me, I will have to radically transform how I take care of myself.

I often think about the woman at the nail-polish station who hurled violent insults at me. What did she need? What was she missing? I'm sure there were countless things: family structure, a safe home, medicine, money. When I am overcome with anger or sadness, I sometimes feel I am that woman. There is a voice inside me that is her voice. I understand her violence, her lack of control, her disgust. In those moments of despair and rage I wonder what she needs.

July 4, 2018, was a hot day in Los Angeles. It was the middle of a heat wave, and even in our air-conditioned apartment it was difficult to sleep at night. That month, the GOP administration began separating children from their families at the US border. I did not feel good about America, so on Independence Day I did what I often do when in the midst of an existential slump: I made care packets for homeless people. Gensan and I spent the morning making sandwiches and stuffing fruit roll-ups, bottled water, and various hygiene products into plastic bags. After a few hours of preparation, we got into the car in the blazing heat and drove to Skid Row. Gensan parked in front of the women's center and we got out of the car, carrying the care packets in our hands.

The packets were gone in about thirty seconds.

Not for the first time, I wondered what to do about the poverty and mental illness around me.

Ten years ago, when I was in India on a Buddhist study-abroad program, I had the opportunity to meet the Karmapa, one of the main reincarnating authority figures in Tibetan Buddhism and head of one of the largest denominations. At the time, he was only about twenty years old — the same age I was. The study-abroad group and I gathered in the Karmapa's ornate meeting chamber. To my surprise, rather than acting compassionate and expansive, the Karmapa seemed grumpy, restless, and uncomfortable.

A question-and-answer session ensued. Someone from our group asked, "How can I be a good Buddhist?"

The Karmapa scowled. "Don't try to be a good Buddhist. Go home to your country and be a good citizen, a good family member, a good neighbor. Work on doing good in your community. Don't worry about Buddhism."

At the time, I thought he was just being cynical. I thought this was a cop-out answer from a young monk who resented the position he was born into. I now understand what he meant.

What will you do with the hours in your day? How will you treat your heart and the people around you? How will you care for your house and the houses around you? These are questions that our lives continually pose for us, no matter where we are, no matter how fucked-up or enlightened we are. In the East or the West, they are wonderful questions to engage. The best place to find the answers is right where you are, right now.

Zen is famous for its enigmatic riddles and jokes. An empty cup is better than a full cup, because you can fill it with anything. Failure is the mother of success. Mind and body are not one, not two. These may seem confusing at first, but they are descriptions of reality. This isn't Zen; this is how things are. Nothing cast away is truly trash. What is unlovable deserves love and belonging. Leftovers and old vegetables are new dinner. You must embrace paradox to transform yourself and your life, to create possibility from nothingness. *End means beginning.*

EPILOGUE

Don't Look in
Other People's Bowls

At Toshoji, we would eat all meals in silence at a table. I remember how hard these meals were for me when I was a layperson, still struggling to adjust to the tastes of Japanese food and the rhythms of *oryoki*. At Buddhist monasteries you are required to eat whatever is put in front of you — whether you are a vegetarian, whether you hate certain things like fish or pumpkins or mushrooms. I often struggled to finish my meals, but I did.

One lunch I was served a food I liked, and I was happy (it may have been cold vegetables with tofu dressing, but I don't remember). I heard the monk beside me munching away and looked over at him. Had he been served more food than me? Suddenly my pleasure turned to jealousy as I saw what I suspected to be a larger serving in his bowl. The abbot of the monastery looked at me from the head of the table. When the meal ended he spoke to the whole group of assembled monks and the lone American girl.

"Dogen said not to look in other people's bowls. Just focus on your own food."

Three years after returning to America from Japan, I have

made a small, strange life for myself. I live with my husband and our two dogs in a tiny, overpriced apartment in San Francisco. We have a living room with a white couch, a green rug, and lots of Japanese calligraphy, including the one I gave him when we first met. We have a small porch overlooking our backyard, with a modest view of downtown and the ocean. I have my own study, which is filled with books on Zen and Japanese history, contemporary novels, and poetry. I sometimes sit there in the morning, but mostly I work full-time with children on the autism spectrum. I am in my second master's program in three years, training to be a marriage and family therapist. I love this program, the rich connections I have made with classmates, and the readings on human emotion, aliveness, and relationships.

And I still suffer. When I look at social media, I see my friends from college buying houses, having children, or making partner in their law firm. I have done none of these things. I feel behind, perhaps to the point where I can never catch up. I have no retirement to speak of. Sometimes when I type out my résumé, I have to laugh. Five years training as a Zen nun. Special skills: chanting, cooking, sweeping.

My pain increases when I compare myself to others, when I look into their bowls. Comparing myself to my peers, I feel like a failure. I do not have their money or their things. I don't have their job titles. But if I can stay still in the unique unfolding of my own life, if I can focus on my own meal, then I do not feel this type of pain. Knowing my life for what it is, I understand that although I am not rich in money, I am rich in love and struggle and seeking. I have valued truth and placed it at the center of my life. My family is near me. I have a refrigerator stocked with food, and a comfortable bed.

Sometimes I am caught breathless at how beautiful this city is. San Francisco is my home, where I was born, where I had my first kiss, where I was married and now live. I love my city — how the light reflects off skyscrapers and the ocean, how the roses look and smell on my block, the way the countless Chinese markets and taquerias beckon.

I remember walking through the countryside in Japan and marveling at the simple beauty of the houses, the bamboo on the hillside, the rich, deep brown of autumn leaves. I remember feeling fierce joy at the sun above me, at the flowers, and at how the mist gathered in the valley below my teacher's mountain temple. I remember loving those mountains. I love my city with the same fierce joy, even as it changes around me.

It is said that when we make this very place our own, our practice becomes the manifestation of truth. This path, this place, is neither big nor small, neither self nor others. This is why we focus on our own bowl, on our own food, on our family and city.

This path, this place, this bowl of food is enough.

ACKNOWLEDGMENTS

This book would not have been possible without the nuns at Aichi Senmon Nisodo in Nagoya, Japan, who educated and encouraged me in cooking. In particular, I would like to thank Eko-san, Myotai-san, Chimyo-san, Hosai-san, and Eika-san for their technical corrections, creative ideas, emotional support, and alternately strict and patient training in the kitchen.

A big thank-you to my husband, Gensan, who smiled and cheered through many experiments in Japanese food, even though it is not his favorite, as well as many, many trips to Japanese restaurants and markets. I am particularly grateful for his coaching in time management and making schedules — a skill I did not have until this year!

Thank you to Georgia Hughes, at New World Library, and Alice Peck for insightful and eye-opening feedback.

GLOSSARY

Common Japanese Ingredients

The recipes in this book include both Japanese and non-Japanese ingredients. Learning to cook good Japanese food involves learning the names and characteristics of a few Japanese vegetables, soy products, and sauces. Some of the following ingredients may be familiar to you, like miso and tofu, while others are perhaps more obscure. Finding a good Asian market will be crucial for obtaining some of these (like *koyadofu*, which I have yet to see in a non-Asian grocery), whereas other foods are easily obtainable in an average grocery store.

abura age: Thinly sliced tofu that has been deep-fried. This is sold in Asian groceries, usually with two to four (2-square-inch) pieces per package. It has a wonderful golden yellow color and makes any dish taste better (in my opinion), especially since traditional temple food uses very little oil normally. *Abura age* is usually cut into thin slices and added to soups and stewed vegetable dishes, although it can also be served whole, simmered in a sweet soy sauce.

atsu age: Thick fried tofu that is soft yet will hold up and not disintegrate in stews. If you can find it at an Asian market, it will have a brown, fried outside and white interior. You can also substitute a Western version, such as tofu cutlets.

daikon: A giant white radish. Daikon are hearty root vegetables that proliferate in the winter, when other vegetables cannot grow. Unless they are sliced very thin, daikon taste too bitter to eat without boiling them first. Afterward they taste like whatever flavoring you add. They can also be grated and used as a garnish for noodle soup or on fried foods such as tempura and deep-fried eggplant (I've heard that grated daikon helps the body digest oil, but that may be an old wives' tale). Don't be surprised to see daikon that are a foot long in stores, but they are sometimes sold in smaller pieces.

dashi: Japanese soup stock that gives food a fishy, salty, umami taste (see chapter 3). Most Japanese make dashi by adding mass-produced dashi powder to hot water, although some home cooks make it the traditional way by boiling bonito or salmon flakes and then straining the liquid. Although dashi is usually made with fish, it can also be prepared a vegetarian way, from kelp and mushrooms. When I speak of dashi in this book I am referring to either home-made stock prepared with *konbu* (dried kelp) and shiitake mushrooms or the powdered vegetarian kind. Please note that homemade dashi is much more subtle (some would say flavorless) than instant.

dengaku or *miso dengaku*: A sweet and salty paste made from mixing together miso, sugar, and mirin or sake. This is then heated in a pan and stirred until the ingredients are combined and the sauce thickens. *Miso dengaku* is often a topping for grilled eggplant, cooked daikon, or other vegetable dishes. It can be made with any miso paste; although darker, red miso is perhaps the most delicious base. It can also be mixed with yuzu (Japanese lemon) or aromatic herbs for a twist on the classic taste.

enoki: Thin white mushrooms (also called "needle mushrooms") that come in tight bunches about 3 inches long. It's not necessary to separate each mushroom from the others, although you can use your hands to break up the bundle a bit. Cut into inch-long pieces, enoki mushrooms taste delicious in miso and other soups.

eryngii: A thicker, taller mushroom than its delicate mushroom counterparts, eryngii are delicious sliced up and fried in butter. They have a heartier, meatier taste than enoki or shimeji, yet are not quite as strong as shiitakes.

fu: High-protein wheat gluten. There are many kinds of *fu*. It can be sold in squares or rectangles, which have a chewy consistency, as small balls that puff up a bit when reconstituted in water or broth, or in pieces that look like sliced baguette (I honestly thought *fu* was dried bread for the first six months I lived in Japan!). Traditionally, there are both raw (fresh) and dry (fried) *fu*, although sadly I have yet to find raw *fu* sold in the United States, even in Asian grocery stores. Recipes in this book call for dried *fu* (also known as *yaki fu*). Because *fu* absorbs the flavor of the sauce around it, it is particularly delicious in soup or in saucy dishes such as *sukiyaki* (Winter Hot Pot, p. 60) and vegetarian *niku jyaga* (Meat 'n' Potatoes for Zen Monks, p. 24).

ginkgo nuts: Ginkgo nuts are delicacies in Japan. Squishy and light green, with a delicious texture and bittersweet taste, these nuts are versatile and often show up in egg custard, stir-fries, or all by themselves as a salty snack.

gobo: Burdock root. *Gobo* are usually sold in bundles and can be up to 3 feet long! They need to be thoroughly washed before using, as they often have a large quantity of dirt stuck to them. You can also use a wire sponge to scrape off excess dirt. *Gobo* are inedible when raw and should be soaked in water with a little bit of vinegar before cooking to remove bitterness and soften them. This also prevents them from discoloring (similar to the way cut potatoes darken when exposed to air).

hijiki: A kind of edible seaweed that looks a bit like black rice when reconstituted. It has a sweet taste vaguely reminiscent of licorice. It is often served stewed and mixed with soybeans and other vegetables.

kabocha: Japanese pumpkin (*Cucurbita maxima*), a different species than the Western counterpart (*Cucurbita pepo*). Don't try to make the dishes in this book with an American pumpkin! Kabocha is small and round with sweet flesh. The green skin is actually edible, although it is often beveled with a knife to create an aesthetically pleasing pattern.

katakuriko: Potato starch. In Japan, potato starch is used in place of cornstarch. However, they are practically interchangeable.

komatsuna: A green vegetable with a crisp stalk and leaves that range from 3 to 7 inches long and 1 inch to 2 inches wide, described to me by a monk as "spinach's Japanese cousin." Like spinach, it is perfect in soup, in *aemono* (mixed salads), or to add color to *nimono* (stew). You can find it in Asian grocery stores, or simply substitute spinach, although this will not produce the brilliant bright green color and crunch of *komatsuna*.

konbu: A kind of edible kelp. There are many varieties of Japanese kelp, but for the purposes of this book, the kelp you need for making soup stock is flat, hard, and dark brown or blackish green. Look for the biggest pieces you can find, as they will be thick and full of flavor. Good *konbu* is coated with a thin layer of white powder. Many recipes instruct you to wash this off first, which is actually a bad idea, because the white powder holds the most umami flavor.

konnyaku: A gray gelatinous cake made from the corm of a taro-like Asian potato called konjak or devil's tongue, which often comes in large blocks about 7 × 4 inches. It has a rubbery texture, which I have heard unflatteringly compared to a "car tire." It also smells! Fun times. To remove the smell, the *konnyaku* is boiled for a few minutes before being added to dishes, usually stews.

koyadofu: Freeze-dried tofu. Available in Japanese markets or online, *koyadofu* is white and when reconstituted in water has the texture of a sponge. Some Westerners are put off by the sponginess, but I quite like how the texture allows it to absorb liquid and flavor. When I was first living in Japan, I read that *koyadofu* originated when a monk left tofu outside overnight in the winter. Inspired by this story, I tried to slice and freeze my own tofu, which, not surprisingly, failed spectacularly. Buy the packaged kind!

mirin: Sweet rice wine that is ubiquitous in Japanese cooking. If you have access to a well-stocked grocery store, you probably don't even need to go to an Asian market to find it. According to *Bon Appétit* magazine, you can substitute dry sherry or Marsala, although I wouldn't add Italian wine to Japanese food. If I'm out of mirin, I usually mix sugar into sake at a ratio of about 1 part sugar to 4 parts sake.

miso: Japanese fermented soybean paste, sold in a plastic tub in most grocery stores. If possible, find a Japanese product rather than an American-made brand. Miso can be white, red, or yellow, although for miso soup yellow miso is your best bet. You can also combine kinds — for example, half white and half red. I've heard that miso never goes bad, but I have yet to test that theory.

miso dengaku: See "*dengaku* or *miso dengaku*."

mitsuba: A flavorful herb, like parsley, that is used in clear soups and as garnish. It has a slightly bitter yet pleasing fresh taste.

mochi: A glutinous rice cake. Mochi usually appears in stores as small white disks or squares. In a good Asian grocery store you can find it in the freezer or packaged and ready to use. Mochi is chewy and can be grilled, which makes it puff up. It is often used in desserts as well. Mochi is a very auspicious food and is placed on Japanese altars at New Year's.

moyashi: Japanese mung bean sprouts, which are white and about 3 inches long; they come 2 to 3 cups to a package. Blanching takes under 2 minutes, or they can be added to stir-fries at the end.

nasu: Japanese eggplant. It is smaller and thinner than American and European eggplant, but is used the same way.

natto: Fermented soybeans that are infamously smelly and sticky and a challenge for non-Japanese to eat. Usually sold in white Styrofoam cases, they come with a sweet soy seasoning and mustard.

nira: Garlic chives, commonly used in Japanese, Chinese, and Korean cooking.

nori: A type of thin, dried edible (and delicious) seaweed not to be confused with *konbu*. If you've ever eaten a sushi roll, you've eaten nori, the black seaweed casing. Nori is used to wrap rice balls or often shredded and used as a garnish on noodle dishes. It can also be a crunchy snack straight from the package.

okara: The pulp of soybeans that remains after tofu is made. *Okara* is usually simmered with dashi, shiitakes, carrots, *abura age*, soy sauce, and sugar, although it can also be a meat substitute if you get a bit creative. I've read that Japanese tofu shops produce around 15 gallons of *okara* daily. Since it is technically considered waste, it is sold quite cheaply in large bags in Japanese markets (check the re-frigerated section where the tofu is located). It looks kind of like crushed popcorn or cottage cheese. Be careful to freeze your leftovers and don't keep it in the refrigerator for more than a few days.

panko: Japanese bread crumbs. They are used in a similar fash-ion as Italian bread crumbs, but are larger and harder, making the food they coat crunchy. These days you can find *panko* in most grocery stores.

ponzu sauce: Soy sauce flavored with yuzu or other citrus. A common Japanese condiment, ponzu sauce is great on tofu products, or simply steam vegetables and douse them with ponzu. You'll thank me.

renkon: Lotus root, so named for the beautiful flowerlike pat-tern of holes that is revealed after slicing the root. *Renkon* is white, delicate, and used in stir-fries, soups, and stews. Peel the *renkon* with a carrot peeler and thinly slice or cut it into bite-size pieces. Soak the *renkon* in water with a little bit of vinegar for at least 10 minutes before using.

sake: Wine made from fermented rice. (In Japanese, sake lit-erally means "alcohol.") Like using Italian wine in recipes, it's good to cook with a high-quality sake that you'd enjoy drinking by itself. However, most Asian grocery stores sell "cooking sake" that is cheaper than drinking sake and fine to use in recipes. Sake deepens the flavor of stews and can be mixed with sugar and other ingredients to make mar-inades and sauces. Considering the prohibition against drinking alcohol in Buddhist temples, I sure learned to cook with a lot of sake! I'm under the impression that most of the alcohol burns away as it cooks.

sansho: An aromatic herb often used as a garnish and in soup or ground into a powder. With its thin stem lined with two rows of symmetrical, tiny leaves, it is ubiquitous in pho-tographs of Japanese food and in expensive restaurants.

shiitake mushrooms: Flavorful, savory mushrooms with large brown caps (1 to 3 inches) and white stalks. These can be purchased fresh, in which case they are fleshy and formidable mushrooms that can be sliced and added to stir-fries, grilled, or stewed. The dried variety is sold in plastic packages in most Asian grocery stores or online. These need to be reconstituted in water (overnight is best), and the flavorful, pungent soaking liquid can be used in stock. Dried shiitakes have a much stronger flavor than fresh ones, so they are not often used interchangeably.

shimeji mushrooms: Mushrooms with brown caps and white stalks, similar to but a little bit thicker than enoki. Their uses are almost interchangeable though — both are great in soup. If using in soup, break the shimeji up with your hands and cut into inch-long pieces or cook whole. Since shimeji are a little heartier than enoki, you can also use them in stew, especially if you don't separate the stalks and cook them in inch-wide clusters. Shimeji and enoki are both sold in Asian supermarkets.

shirataki: Thin "noodles" made of *konnyaku* most commonly found in *sukiyaki* and other stews or in vinegared dishes with cucumber. Like *konnyaku*, they also have zero calories and, not surprisingly, very little taste. In stews they add a nice crunch.

shiso: A diamond-shaped green herb with frayed edges that is often called "Japanese basil," though it is also reminiscent of mint. Its uses are similar to those for both mint and basil (but they are not substitutes for each other!). Sliced thin, it is a powerful flavoring and garnish. *Shiso* can be found in Asian groceries, although in my experience a Japanese grocery is more likely to carry it than a Korean or Chinese one.

soy sauce: A dark liquid made from fermented soybeans. Tamari is a kind of soy sauce that is made without wheat, making it a useful soy sauce substitute for people with gluten intolerance.

takenoko: The young shoots of the bamboo plant. These proliferate in Japan in the springtime. Perhaps this is an obvious thing to state, but you cannot substitute an older bamboo plant (which is a tree) for a bamboo shoot, which is tender and pliable. Bamboo shoots are delicious sliced thin in soups or as bigger pieces simmered in broth. Bamboo can be purchased preboiled and cleaned in Japanese markets.

tare: "Dipping sauce," but the term also refers to the strong, distinctive foundation of ramen broth. Common kinds of ramen *tare* are *sio*, miso, and *soyu*. Each ramen chef probably comes up with a distinctive *tare* to give the ramen broth its flavor.

tofu: White soybean curd that is formed into blocks with a texture that in Japan is either soft (silken) or firm. Silken tofu is best in soup, and firm tofu is good in stir-fries or stews or deep-fried (silken tofu will be destroyed in that kind of heat). I've discovered that Americans seem to prefer firm tofu over the silken kind, but there is nothing quite like a high-quality soft tofu on a hot day served with a drizzle of soy sauce, grated ginger, and sliced green onions. If you are ever in Kyoto, make sure to get yudofu (cooked tofu) from a restaurant in the temple complex of Nanzenji.

wakame: Thin edible seaweed that is often used in soup. In Japan, the best quality wakame is fresh and packed in salt, although dried wakame is easier to find in the West. For 1 cup of soup, 1 teaspoon or so of dried wakame should suffice — it expands in the water. Also be aware that adding wakame will increase the salt content, so it's better to taste for salt after adding the wakame.

yuzu: A citrus fruit (*Citrus junos*), often called a "Japanese lemon," that is much smaller than a lemon, closer to a tangerine in size. Yuzu are, in my experience, sweeter and less tart than lemons. Thinly sliced, the peel is delightful as a garnish, in soups, or to flavor *dengaku* sauce. Substituting yuzu for lemon is a little tricky. I wouldn't use the two interchangeably in something like soup, where the flavor subtleties are really pronounced, but it is probably fine to use lemon instead of yuzu in some sauces.

Useful Equipment

It is not necessary to purchase special equipment for the recipes in this book. Most of the dishes can be made with improvised tools. However, the following are traditional Japanese cooking tools that will make certain steps far easier.

electric rice cooker: A modern device that will save a lot of time and energy. I've found that the quality of rice made in an electric rice cooker is actually a lot better than that made on the stovetop.

ginger grater: A small metallic Japanese grater that is flat with very fine teeth for grating ginger, which is used as a garnish for fried tofu, eggplant, and noodle soup. This tool won't completely liquefy the ginger as you grate it, as other graters do. It's also useful for grating citrus peel.

handai or *sushi oke*: A large circular bamboo bowl that has a flat bottom and is a good shape to mix rice in to cool it down or just to serve it in a pleasing way, especially when making a large dish of mixed rice or sushi rice (such as Colorful "Sushi" Rice, p. 37). Of course, you could use a regular serving dish, but rice served in a traditional bamboo bowl is particularly satisfying.

miso paste muddler/strainer: A tool used to properly mix miso into soup stock. It allows the best-tasting part of the miso to dissolve into the soup while catching the chunkier pieces. Although certain Western tools (such as a very fine colander) may work, a normal colander with large holes will let the miso's chunkier soybean pieces fall back into the soup.

suribachi: The Japanese version of a mortar and pestle, useful for grinding sesame seeds or mashing tofu and other vegetables, such as mountain yam. The bowl is usually ceramic, with fine grooves inside, and the pestle is made of wood.

Popular Japanese Cooking Techniques

aemono: "Mixed salads." Although not really a technique, *aemono* are an integral part of Japanese meals (*ae* means "mixed" and *mono* means "things"). *Aemono* are usually small portions of mixed vegetables that complement a larger, heartier dish. A senior nun at Nisodo told me that a good rule of thumb is no more than three kinds of vegetables at a time; "otherwise it looks like dog food." Those three, however, can be virtually any combination of ingredients, and in this cookbook I have included recipes for Cold Vegetables with Tofu Dressing (p. 43) and Cucumber and Bean Sprout Salad (p. 82).

agedashi: A method of cooking, much like using a Western marinade, in which the vegetable or protein is deep-fried and then placed in a rich, sweet soy broth. It's one of my favorite ways of preparing food (what's not to like about deep-fried tofu bathing in a bowl of hot savory broth?). There are two kinds of *agedashi* in this book, Marinated Fried Eggplant (p. 95) and Fried Tofu in Sauce (p. 57).

itamemono: A term meaning "fried," but usually referring to a mixture of stir-fried vegetables.

itameni: A combination of two cooking methods, frying (*itame*) and stewing (*ni*). *Itameni* dishes often contain the same ingredients as *nimono*, for example, potatoes, carrots or daikon, and fried tofu. However, instead of boiling the vegetables first, in this method the vegetables are lightly sautéed first. Then broth is added to the frying pan and the vegetables are cooked all the way through in the soy-sugar mixture. It's a more flavorful, if perhaps clumsier, version of *nimono*. There are many such stews in this book.

nimono: A method I translate as "stewed" or "simmered," although it refers to a particular procedure that involves boiling vegetables, usually heavy root vegetables such as carrots, potatoes, or daikon, and then simmering or soaking them in a sweet soy broth. In *nimono* it's important to boil the vegetables first without any flavor, even salt. Adding them to the hot broth after boiling allows the vegetables to absorb the flavor of the soy sauce and sugar with little or no warping or discoloring the skin or flesh. *Nimono* produces subtle dishes that are comforting and no-frills.

sunomono: A salad of any kind of vegetable with a vinegar dressing (*sunomono* means "vinegar thing"), usually with some sugar and a tiny bit of soy sauce. *Sunomono* are usually small side dishes that pair with larger stews and stir-fries. Julienned Daikon and Carrot in Sweet Vinegar Sauce (p. 156) and Crushed Cucumber and Tomato Salad (p. 26) are two such dishes.

NOTES

p. 4   *the United States has the highest rate of consumer spending*: "Final Consumption Expenditures," World Bank, https://data .worldbank.org/indicator/NE.CON.TOTL.CD?year_high _desc=false.

p. 4   *the highest military spending budget*: Niall McCarthy, "The Top 15 Countries for Military Expenditure in 2016," *Forbes*, https://www.forbes.com/sites/niallmccarthy/2017/04/24 /the-top-15-countries-for-military-expenditure-in-2016 -infographic/#7176a36843f3.

p. 4   *the highest rate of obesity*: "OECD Obesity Update 2017," http://www.oecd.org/health/obesity-update.htm.

p. 4   *23 percent of the world's coal*: "Use It and Lose It: The Outsize Effect of U.S. Consumption on the Environment," *Scientific American*, https://www.scientificamerican.com/article /american-consumption-habits/.

p. 4   *not having a child decreases her carbon footprint by twenty times*: Kate Galbraith, "Having Children Brings High Carbon Impact," *New York Times*, August 7, 2009, https://green.blogs .nytimes.com/2009/08/07/having-children-brings-high-carbon -impact/.

p. 6   *I read of a study by Princeton University*: Belinda Luscombe, "Do We Need $75,000 a Year to Be Happy?" *Time*, September 6,

2010, http://content.time.com/time/magazine/article/0,9171, 2019628,00.html.

p. 19 *because of the Delboeuf illusion*: Koert Van Ittersum and Brian Wansink, "Plate Size and Color Suggestibility: The Delboeuf Illusion's Bias on Serving and Eating Behavior," *Journal of Consumer Research* 39, no. 2 (2012): 215–28.

p. 20 *"Although the wind / blows terribly here"*: Jane Hirshfield and Mariko Aratani, *The Ink Dark Moon: Love Poems by Ono no Komachi and Izumi Shikibu, Women of the Ancient Court of Japan* (New York: Random House, 1990), p. 124.

p. 48 *the fear of MSG health risks stems from one letter*: Caitlin Dewey, "Why Americans Still Avoid MSG, Even Though Its 'Health Effects' Have Been Debunked," *Washington Post*, March 20, 2018, https://www.washingtonpost.com/news/wonk/wp/2018/03/20 /why-americans-still-avoid-msg-even-though-its-health-effects -have-been-debunked/?utm_term=.973d050fd274.

p. 48 *researchers now believe the myth of MSG health risks persists because*: Dewey, "Why Americans Still Avoid MSG."

p. 49 *Researchers also note that our culture*: Dewey, "Why Americans Still Avoid MSG."

p. 75 *"We may have been taught that experiences we have at the 'spiritual' level"*: Jack Kornfield, *A Path with Heart* (New York: Random House, 1999), p. 246.

p. 76 *"Because awareness does not automatically transfer itself"*: Kornfield, *A Path with Heart*, p. 249.

p. 132 *"Japan's multicultural gastronomy helped nurture a modern mass society"*: Eric Han, *Rise of a Japanese Chinatown: Yokohama, 1894–1972* (Cambridge, MA: Harvard University Asia Center, 2014), p. 96.

p. 133 *"If I wanted to make a bowl of ramen that was personal to me"*: Ivan Orkin, *Ivan Ramen: Love, Obsession, and Recipes from Tokyo's Most Unlikely Noodle Joint* (Berkeley, CA: Ten Speed Press, 2013), p. 108.

INDEX

ABOUT THE
AUTHOR

Gesshin Claire Greenwood is the author of *Bow First, Ask Questions Later: Ordination, Love, and Monastic Zen in Japan* and the popular blog *That's So Zen*. Ordained as a Buddhist nun in Japan in 2010, she trained in Zen monasteries for several years, during which time she apprenticed in the kitchen under Japanese Buddhist nuns. Eventually she trained as *tenzo* (head chef), serving traditional Buddhist vegan and vegetarian food to temple members and guests. She received Dharma transmission (permission to teach) in 2015. A fiery, insatiable, and rebellious feminist, she eventually decided cloistered convent life was not for her and returned to the United States, obtaining a master's degree in East Asian studies from the University of Southern California. She currently lives with her husband and two dogs in San Francisco, where she cooks, teaches meditation, and works in the mental-health field. Her religion is kindness, truth, and good food.